INTERNATIONAL LAW

BY THE SAME AUTHOR

International Politics
International Relations

INTERNATIONAL LAW

P. CHANDRA

Head, Department of Political Science
B.S.M. (P.G.) College, Roorkee

VIKAS PUBLISHING HOUSE PVT LTD

VIKAS PUBLISHING HOUSE PVT LTD
Regd. Office: 5 Ansari Road, New Delhi 110002
Head Office: **Vikas House, 20/4 Industrial Area, Sahibabad 201010**
Distt. Ghaziabad, U.P. (India)

Printed at Chetna Printers, A-27/2A, Shastri Marg, Maujpur Delhi-110053

Preface

The present study of International Law is a sequel to two earlier titles—*Internatianal Politics* and *International Relations*—so as to complete a modest trilogy of international affairs.

Following the established pattern, the study has been divided into two parts—Part I covering the Law of Peace and Part II that of War and Neutrality, and is followed by leading cases on International Law. In 26 chapters all important principles and norms of International Law have been thoroughly examined.

Keeping the substance of the subject-matter intact, a deliberate attempt has been made to do away with unnecessary details with a view to make the study more compact, coherent and concise. In view of a general complaint received from the students regarding the cumbersome commentaries and bulky books, an effort has been made to condense as far as possible the colossal material available on the subject and to present it in a fairly comprehensive yet sufficiently handy form.

Written for the post-graduate students of Political Science and Law of various universities and other competitive examinations like IAS & IPS, it will be useful for general reeders interested in world affairs.

In this context the author wishes to record his sense of indebtedness to some excellent titles on International Law, such as *International Law* by Oppenheim; *International Law* by Fenwick; *An Introduction to International Law* by Starke; *Principles of International Law* by Lawrence; *The Law of Nations* by Brierly; *Theory and Reality of International Law* by Visscher; *A Modern Introduction to International Law* by Michael Akehurst; *Manual of Public International Law* by M. Sorensen; *Public International Law* by M.P. Tandon; *Public International Law* by V.D. Mahajan; and *International Law* by Sobhan Lal Mookerjea. In making special mention of these works the author wishes to acknowledge his heavy reliance on them for preparing the material of this volume.

Besides, the pains taken by Shri S.P. Sharma for undertaking the job of typing without pleading pressure of time are also acknowledged.

Above all, I am highly grateful to VIKAS for bringing out this book within a short time. Suggestions for further improvement of the book are earnestly invited and shall be gratefully acknowleged.

P. CHANDRA

Contents

PART I: LAW OF PEACE

PART I

LAW OF PEACE

Chapter 1

Nature and Scope of International Law

The term international law was coined in 1780 by Jeremy Bentham, the great utilitarian of England.

Oppenheim has defined international law as "the name for the body of customary and conventional rules which are considered legally binding by civilized states in their intercourse with one another."[1] In the words of Fenwick, it is "the body of rules accepted by the general community of nations as defining their rights and the means of procedure by which those rights may be protected or violations of them redressed."[2]

According to Brierly, "it is the body of rules and principles of action which are binding upon civilized states in their relations with one another."[3] To paraphrase these definitions, international law is the sum total of rules, principles, customs, and agreements which states accept as having the force of law for the regulation of phases of international relations. To quote an Indian writer, Subimal Mukerjee, "it is a law for equitable and just regulation of international relations within world community."[4] Starke, however, has offered a much wider, comprehensive and satisfactory definition of international law: "It is that body of law which states feel themselves bound to observe and therefore do commonly observe in their relations with each other and which includes also: (*a*) the rules of law relating to the functioning of international institutions or organisations, their relations with each other and their relations with states and individuals ; (*b*) certain rules of law relating to individuals and non-state entities so far as the rights and duties of such individuals and non-state entites are the concern of international community."[5] Dr Jessup and Professor McDougal also draw our attention to the expanding nature of international law. In sum, international law is a body of generally accepted principles and rules controlling the conduct of national states, non-state entities, international organisations, individuals and corporations.

NATURE OF INTERNATIONAL LAW

Whether international law is 'law' in the true sense has been a subject of constant debate among jurists. Regarding the nature of international law, some writers, like Zimmer and Willoughby have grave doubts as to whether it is a law or not. Since international law does not appear to restrain or even affect states in their actual pursuit of 'Vital national interest', which are often narrow and selfish, doubts are often expressed that international law is really law at all.

To the Austinian School, it is not a true law. It is nothing but international morality consisting of opinions and sentiments prevailling among sovereign nations of the world. It is not binding as it is unsupported by the authority of a state. It is not backed by any overwhelming sanctions against potential law breakers. It is thus a branch of International morality having only a moral force. Thinkers like Hobbes, Pufendorf, Austin, Holland, Zimmern, Willughby, etc., belong to this School of jurisprudence. Holland even went to the extent of calling it as 'the vanishing point of jurisprudence'. For him it is 'law' by courtesy only, because it has only moral sanction and no teeth. What he means to say is that international law is a diminishing dot on the legal horizon.

But, on the other hand, modern writers like Hall, Lawrence, Oppenheim, etc., maintain that international law not only operates as law but is distinct from international morality both with regard to the nature of its rules as well as its sanctions. Oppenheim however admits that international law is cooparatively a weaker law, because 'it is a law between and not above the state'.

Now the question is how to reconcile the views of the Austinian School and the modern jurisprudence. As a matter of fact the controversy rests upon the definition of law which one may choose to adopt. Austin would not accept it as true law because it is not the will of a political superior. Holland would reject it as law because it cannot be enforced by a sovereign political authority. To these writers, law implies a law giver and a tribunal capable of enforcing it and coercing its transgressors. Thus those who measure international law by national or municipal law believe that absence of centralized legislature, executive and judicial authority disqualified it as true law. But if Oppenheim's definition is accepted as the true measure of law, all doubts whether international law is law or not are removed. He defines law "as a body of rules for human conduct within a community which by common consent of this community shall be enforced by external power."[6] Now the family of nations may be regarded as international community where have grown certain rules to govern inter-state conduct and the enforcement of these rules is sanctioned by the consent of international community.

The only essential conditions for the existence of law are the existence of a political community and recognition by its members of settled rules binding upon them in that capacity. International law seems to satisfy these conditions to an ample extent.

Modern jurisprudence discounts force and formal legislative authority. Today laws bear less and less the character of command and acquire more and more the character of customary law founded on consent. To Hall and Lawrence it is law in the proper sense. It is habitually treated and enforced as law. Like certain kind of positive law it is derived from custom, and precedents do form its source and the observance of its rules is not voluntary. Its rules are compulsory and rest in the last resort on force though exerted through irregular action of international society. As a matter of fact the adequacy of law is a function of its acceptability, its just nature and its enforceability. International law like municipal law passes this three-fold test.

WEAKNESSES OF INTERNATIONAL LAW

The fact that a law of nations exists must not blind us to the fact that it is still a relatively weak law. International law does suffer from certain weaknesses. It lacks a coherent body of codified law. The absence of obligatory judicial settlement is another weakness. It also lacks a centralized executive authority. In short, the international legal system lacks institutional support. Its sanctions therefore work less effectively. It is less imperative and lacks the coercive force of state law. It has no legal power to enforce its decisions. Moreover, there is no organised public opinion to sustain it. Thus, to quote Prof. Paton, "International law is very weak on the institutional side." However, what is crucial is not the absence of legislature or International Parliament but obligatory judicial settlement and centralized executive authority. Another defect is that the international organisation has no jurisdiction over domestic matters. The UN cannot interfere in matters which are essentially within the domestic jurisdiction of any state. Consequently when grave issues arise we see flagrant disregard of accepted rules. Other limitations are imprecision of legal norms, obsolescence of legal principles due to slow changes, absence of legal standards for regulating some new phenomenon such as exploitation and mining of sea-bed of the high seas, subversion, hijacking and another forms of terrorism. But it is noteworthy that states breaking it never deny the existence of international law. They do recognize its reality through an endeavour to interpret it as justifying their conduct. "While the frequency of the violation of international law may strain its legal force to breaking point, the formal though cynical affirmation of its binding nature is not without significance." All told, states may violate international law but no more than individuals. Further, whenever states defend their violations they never claim that they are above law.[7] Almost without exception, when states violate international law or show wayward behaviour, they refrain from denying its existence; instead they find excuses and alibis of many kinds and thereby try to make their actions appear legal.[8] Thus in spite of some spectacular exceptions we can safely say that most nations have observed most of international law most of the time.

REFERENCES

1. OPPENHEIM, L., *International Law*, H. Lauterpacht (ed), London, Longman, Vol. 1, 8th Edition, 1966, pp. 4-5.
2. FENWICK, C.G., *International Law*, New York, Appleton, Century-Crofts, 1924, p. 34.
3. BRIERLY, J.L., *The Law of Nations*, H. Waldock (ed), London, Oxford University Press, 6th Ed., 1963, p. 1.
4. MUKHERJEE SUBIMAL in Sobhan Lal Mookerjea, *International Law*, Calcutta, A. Mukherjee & Co, Vol. I, 2nd Ed., 1968, p. 5.
5. STARKE J.G., *An Introduction to International Law*, London, Butterworths, 7th Ed., 1972, p. 1.
6. OPPENHEIM in M.P. Tandon, *Public International Law*, Allahabad, Allahabad Law Agency, 15th Ed., 1976, p. 10.
7. BRIERLY in M.P. Tandon, *Public International Law*, op. cit., p. 11.
8. OPPENHEIM, *International Law*, op, cit., pp. 14-15.

Chapter 2

Sources and Sanctions of International Law

The problem of sources of law is of great theoretical and practical importance as it has to answer to question how the norms of international law orginate and how to find them. According to Lawrence, if the source means beginning with all the authority to give it binding force then there is one source only; the consent of nations whether tacit (customs) or express (treaties).[1] Oppenheim also shares the same view. According to him, "treaties and customs must be regarded as the exclusive source of the Law of Nations."[2] However, at present the Statute of International Court of Justice is an authoritative text of the sources and evidences of international law. Article 38 of the statute stipulates that it shall apply: (1) International conventions; (2) International custom as evidence of a general practice accepted as law; (3) The general principles of law recognised by civilized nations as main sources. The third one, however, is not a substantive source but a kind of formulational or methodological source. It helps the application of a general law to particular cases; (4) Judicial decision; and (5) Techings of publicists as subsidiary means for determining the rules of law. Some minor sources are: International comity, State Papers, Instructions from the Executive, Resolutions of International Conferences, Municipal Acts of Parliament, and Decisions of Municipal Courts and Opinions of Jurisconsults and Textbook writers including the techings and findings of jurists and scholars based on their research, reflection and experience.

1. Treaties

International treaties and conventions are considered to be the most important source of international law. In fact, multinational treaties are a feeble approach to international legislation. Treaties are of course the best means of achieving and maintaining world public order based on international cooperation.

Treaties may be divided into two groups: (1) law making treaties and (2) treaty contracts covering special matter between contracting states only.[3] However, only law making treaties are the source of international law. The law making treaty involves two distinct operations: (*a*) a legislative operation whereby rules are laid down and (*b*) undertaking of contraction parties to conform to the rules. Some of the examples of law making treaties are: (*a*) Various peace treaties such as Treaty of West Phalia (1648), Treaty of Paris (1815) and Treaty of Versailles (1919) creating constitutional Charters; (*b*) Declaration of Paris (1856), Geneva Conventions of 1864, 1906, 1929, and 1949, Suez Canal Convention (1888), the two Hague Conventions of 1899 and 1907, the Convenant of the League of Nations (1920), the Paris Pact (1928), Montreux Convention (1936) and the Charter of the United Nations (1945) which are pure law making treaties. However, it is to be noted that treaty stipulations override rules of international customs. The P.C.I.J. approved this proposition in S.S. Wimbledon case. Even law making treaties at times do not bind states which are not parties to them. Nevertheless the U.N. Charter binds non-members as well.

2. International Customs

Custom is that line of conduct which the society has consented to regard obligatory. It is an implied agreement. Custom is older and original source of international law but it has lost its priority since the middle of the nineteenth century. Any way, it is still the second most important source. Custom is different from usage. Usage represents the twilight stage of custom. Custom begins where usage ends. The test usually adopted in order to ascertain whether usage has developed into obligatory custom is that it must be approved by the common consent of civilized nations.

The predominance of custom in international law is due to loose character of international society. There is no strong central authority to regulate inter-state relations and no effective law making machinery. The existence of a custom, however, requires to be proved. In order to establish an international custom there must be repetition, continuity and generality of a series of analogous facts.[4] There is a growing trend of thought that custom has only a declaratory and not a constitutive character. International custom is therefore defined as evidence of general practice accepted as law.

When a state becomes a member of the international community it automatically subjects itself to customary law of nations. The extraterritorial rights and privileges enjoyed by diplomats, 3 miles limit of territorial waters, until recently, and rules governing international transit by sea and air furnish some of the examples of the force of custom as a basis for international law.

Interaction of treaties and customs. Regarding, their inter-se relationship, in principle it is possible to change the customary norm by means of a treaty (Case of S.S. Wimbledon) and a treaty norm by means of custom (Preah Vihear Temple case).

But in practice treaties and customs are different forms of one essential element—agreement of subjects of international law. They have identical legal force and are mutually reinforcing. Thus as source of international law they do not oppose each other but interact and supplement each other.[5] Hence the question of primacy of treaty or a custom is purely academic. Nevertheless treaties are the best means of achieving and maintaining world public order based on international cooperation.

3. General Principles of Law

General principles are the broadest source of international law. They include basic principles of law which are indisputable, principles of equity and justice and universally accepted principles of construction. They also embrace the principles of private law administered in national course. Incidentally, private law in general is more developed than international law. The incorporation of this clause in the Statute discards the positivist view about international law. It also militates against the view that international law lacks the requisite elasticity to determine international disputes according to the fundamental legal principles. By applying principles of equity fully taking into account the spirit of international law the courts fill the gap in the legal system. To illustrate, the rules of 'prescription' and 'occupation' as found in private law is applied to international sphere also. General principles are more useful in new areas of international law. The main function of the general principles of law has been that of a safety valve to be kept in reserve rather than to source of frequent application.

4. Judicial Decisions

Article 38 of the Statute refers to judicial decisions as a subsidiary means for the determination of rules of law. Judicial decisions are presumed to be merely declaratory as to the existence or interpretation of existing rules of law discovered on an examination of the material clearly sources or evidences of rules. Article 59 provides that it has no binding force except between parties, and even between parties to the dispute it will bind them only in respect of that particular case. The intent is to exclude judicial law-making. Yet judicial decisions have been referred to as manifestation of the intrinsic merits of judicial precedent. Thus the decision of an international court is not itself a rule of international law but is direct evidence of the existence of a rule of law. Although normally precedents are not binding here as in national law, the practice of referring to them has become one of the most consipicuous feature of the judgement and opinions of the courts.

The decisions of municipal courts are not accorded the same sanctity as to those of international courts. They were seldom cited by the two world courts. The decisions of the courts of every country, so far as they are founded upon a law common to every country will be received not as authority but with respect. These courts deal problems concerning tariffs, extradition citizenship, etc. The judicial value of the decisions depend upon their intrinsic worth and their empirical value. The judicial pronouncements of the I.C.J. in the Anglo-Norwegian fisheries case, the Genocide advisory opinion and the North Sea Continental Shelf cases indubitably affirm their normative impact upon the international law commission and other agencies.

5. **Text Writers, Works of Jurists and Commentators**

Article 38 authorizes the court to apply jurists' teachings as subsidiary means. Their writings are not independent source, though they may lead to form international law by providing useful evidence of what the law is. Writers themselves don't make law, but theycrea te law-abiding sentiment, a strong repugnance to the neglect or breach of certain rules regulating the relations and actions of states. The writings of Ayala, Gentiles, Grotius, Vattel, Kent, Zouche Oppenheim, etc., have tended to transform the transitory stage of usage into custom and represented a strong element to consolidate the customary law. These writers are accorded respect because of their impartiality. They may be referred to for the purpose to information and clarification.

The other minor sources of international law are judicial reason, natural law, international comity such as rules of politeness, goodwill convenience and courtesy, international state papers such as foreign office records, states instructions for the guidance of their own officials and Acts of international organizations such as Declaration of Human Rights and Fundamental Freedoms. As regards the legal Status of the Resolution of the General Assembly, it is to be noted that most of them are exhoratory in character. Their force depends upon the extent to which they can be regarded as expression of the judicial conscience of humanity as a whole. They are valuable as subsidiary means for the determination of rules of law.

SANCTIONS OF INTERNATIONAL LAW

"A sanction is an action, ordinarily illegal, permitted by a legal community against a law breaker." It has been pointed out earlier that international law lacks coercive force or sanctions that are available behind national law. Consequently international is less imperative. But in spite of the fact that its sanction work less effectively as compared to that of national law, international law is not without sanctions which work well.

In the international society of today, the binding force of international law is constituted by an aggregate effect of several factors which include mutual respect, reciprocal advantage, fear of retaliation, world public opinion and the odium associated with the law breaker. According to one writer, consideration of expediency, convenience, mutual interest, and moral approbation are the real sanctions of international law. F. Schuman classifies the sanctions in order of their importance as (1) habit, (2) expediency, (3) good faith and (4) organised force.[6]

Some other factors contributing to observance of international law are self interest, balance of power, collective security, guarantee of third party, international court, world public opinion, sanction of international organisation and threat of war. To quote Padelford and Lincoln, "expedience, mutual convenience, respect for the rights of others, prestige, and the possibility of suffering retaliation or being exposed to forceful actions all motivate support and observance of law in relations among sovereign states "[7]

REFERENCES

1. LAWRENCE, T.J., *Principles of International Law*, P.H. Winfield (ed), New York, 1925, p. 95.
2. OPPENHEIM, *International Law*, op. cit., p. 25.
3. STARKE, *An Introduction to International Law*, op. cit., p. 45.
4. TANDON, M.P., *Public International Law*, op. cit., p. 20.
5. SHARMA, SURYA P., "Treaties as a Source of International Law", in *Indian Journal of International Law*, New Delhi, *The Indian Society of International Law*, Vol. 19, No. 4., October-December 1979, p. 510.
6. SCHUMAN F. in M.P. Tandon, *Public International Law*, op. cit., p. 10.
7. PADELFORD, LINCOLN, OLVEY, *Dynamics of International Politics*, New York, Macmillan, 3rd Ed., 1976, p. 448.

Chapter 3

Codification of the Law of Nations

"A code is the consolidation of the Statute law, or a Statute collecting all the law relating to a particular subject."[1] It secures, by means of general conventions, agreements among the States upon certain topics of international law and acts as a check whereby the determination of a particular law is not left to the caprices of judges.

Meanings of Codification

1. Codification means the harmonising of municipal law of various countries by the preparation and enactment of uniform Statutes.

2. It is a systematic restatement of existing customary international law.

3. It also means developing, amending and improving the law as it is restated.

Acticle 15 of the Statute of the International Law Commission distinguishes between the progressive development of international law and its codification. The latter means more precise formulation and systematisation of rules of international law in fields where there already has been extensive state practice, precedent and doctrine. The former means the preparation of draft conventions on subjects which have not yet been regulated by international law or where law has not been sufficiently developed in the practice of states, such as international rules regarding plane hijacking, space low, exploitation of the high seas, etc. However, the two terms are not exclusive and the task of the Commission is to achieve both the purposes.

Advantages of Codification

1. Codification tends to render the law readily ascertainable and to obtain over a large area. There being no efficacious international legal machinery, codification by reconciling conflicting views binds the different units to a large part of law;

2. A carefully closeknit code greatly assists the judge in dispensing justice;

3. The growth of law through custom moves very slowly. The

customary law of a state finds it difficult to keep pace with the advance of civilization. Codification, therefore, becomes a historic necessity to deal with these developments;

4. Disagreement and confusion disappear when the law is codificd;

5. It adds to its clarity and authority and thereby results in the willingness of states to submit obligatory judicial or arbitral settlement;

6. It would fill up numerous lacunae in the existing state of international law and bring uniformity in the system and thus the law would become full and complete; and

7. Lastly, it brings elastisity, simplicity and precision in the rules of international life.

Disadvantages of Codification

Codification, however, is not an unmixed blessing. It suffers from certain disavantages as well:

1. It stereotypes the natural growth of law and cuts off its organic growth. International law, like all law, must be a living, growing, developing organism, for if the conditions change, the rule of law ceases to respond to the requirements of the situation;

2. According to Roscoe Pound "Law must be suitable and yet it cannot be stand-still. The legal order must be flexible as well as stable. It must be over-hauled continually and refitted continually to the changes in the actual life which it is to govern."[2] To quote Cardozo, "the inn that shelters the traveller for the night is not the journey's end. Law like traveller must be ready for the morrow." It must have a principle of growth;

3. It may lead to new and fresh controversies by making the law rigid and inadaptable;

4. Further, international law is still in its infancy: Most of the states still prefer solutions based on political expediency or compromise and are apprehensive of strictly judicial solutions, since they may not conform to the realities of international life; and

5. Lastly, there is a hairsplitting tendency on the part of judges who cling more to the latter than to its spirit. This is another demerit of codified law.

Any way, the advantages for outweigh the demerits of codification. Some of the shortcomings can be obviated, if only those rules are codified which are manifestly in force and a regular revision of the code is maintained. To sum up, codification brings "simplicity, symmetry, intelligibility and logical coherence." The science of law receives a fresh stimulus and if codification is carefully planned and systamatically arranged, many of its disadvantages can be easily avoided.

History of Codification

The idea of codification originated with Jeremy Bentham at the end of the eighteenth century. He suggested a utopian international law for everlasting peace. The first real codification was the Declaration of Paris (1856) which laid down 4 principles. Subsequently codification was attempted by individual writers and some institutes of international law, e.g., Codification by Bluntschli (1868), David Dudley Field (1872), Institute of International Law (1873) and Declaration of Brussels (1874). However, these efforts were of little significance. Codification of any note was made only by two Hague Conference. The First Hague Conference was convened in 1899 which produced 2 covenants mainly dealing with pacific settlement of international disputes and with respect to the laws of war on land. The Second Hague Conference (1907) produced 13 conventions dealing mainly with maritime laws. The unratified Declaration of London (1909) was another notable attempt at codification. Then came the First World War.

The League of Nations established in 1920 took up the task of codification in greater earnest than ever before pursuance of Article 14 of the Covenant. In September 1924 the League Council appointed a Committee of experts to report on the codification of law and to select topics ripe for codification. Consequently seven topics were selected. But the Hague Codification Conference called in 1930 for the purposes failed to make much head way. It could take up only one topic with some success, that of nationality. It adopted conventions relating to conflict of nationality laws, double nationality and stateless persons. Apart from the League efforts, the Washington Conference (1922) attempted at limitation of armanent. In the year 1923, a Commission of Jurists produced a Code of Airwarfare Rules. Again in 1925, a number of states signed a protocol prohibiting use of poisonous gases. Subsequently in 1929 a Conference at Geneva produced a revised convention on the treatment of sick and wounded persons in the field and treatment of war prisoners. Then came the Second World War.

The U.N. Charter and Codification

Article 13 (ix a) of the Charter gives ample scope for Codification. In 1947, an International Law Commission was set up. It consists of

34 members elected by the General Assembly for 5 years. Recently Mr S.P. Jagota from India who has been one of the members of this Commission since 1976 was elected as its Chairman for 1985-86. The work entrusted to this Commission is the promotion of progressive development of international law and its codification. It has to survey the whole field of international law and to select topics for codification. The Commission started its work in 1949. To begin with, 15 topics were given top priority. So far the Commission has succeeded in codifying on the following:

(1) Formulation of Nurumberg Principles. The Commission formulated 7 principles in the light of the Nurumberg Trial; (2) Draft Declaration on Rights and Duties of States in 14 Articles. The Commissioner ultimately formulated 4 Rights and 7 Duties of States; (3) Regime of the High Seas and the Law of the Sea; (4) Diplomatic and Consular Privileges and Immunities; (5) Treaty Law; (6) Arbitral Procedure; (7) Draft Code of Offences against Peace and Security of Mankind; (8) Nationality including Statelessness; (9) Draft on International Criminal Court; (10) Definition of Aggression. A legal committee was entrusted with this task. After sweating at it for about 7 years, it could reach a seeming agreement on a definition of 'aggression' in 1974; and (11) A Draft Convention on Freedom of Information and International Transmission of news has been drawn up.

At present work on 3 topics is in progress. They are: (1) International Responsibility of States; (2) The succession of Governments and States; and (3) Diplomatic law dealing with relations between States and International Organisation, State immunity; International Water Courses; Draft Code of Offences against the Peace and Security of Mankind; the Status of diplomatic courier and diplomatic bag, etc. The most notable achievements of the I.L.C. are Draft on Rights and Duties of States and formulation of Nuremberg Principles. But neither of the two has been approved by sufficient numbers of States.

Future of Codification

The progress of codification work is no doubt slow but perhaps it is due to the nature of its work. However, the subject matter of codification is growing day by day. Hence the problem of codification has become more urgent. Since so many new states have arrived with different legal attitudes and approaches, their divergences can be harmonised only through the efforts of International Law Commission. Of late the General Assembly has been resorting to creation of special Commission and *ad hoc* bodies charged with the drafting of important instructions. For instance, the Human Rights Commission drafted two covenants on Human Rights and the Covention on Genecide. No doubt, the future of codification clearly depends upon conditions more fundamental than the present international relations for which it is sought to formulate specific rules of law.[3] One writer has suggested that there should be a combination of national and international efforts to make the work of codification more fruitful.

REFERENCES

1. TANDON, M.P., *Public International Law*, op. cit., p. 45.
2. POUND, R. in M.P. Tandon, *Public International Law*, op. cit., p. 47.
3. FENWICK, C.G., *International Law*, Bombay, Vakils, Feffer and Simons, 3rd Indian re-print, 1981, p. 105.

Chapter 4

Relation between International Law and Municipal Law

The relationship between municipal law and international law is both of theoretical and practical interest. There is constent interaction between the two systems of law, and each has reciprocal impact on the other. International law governs the relations of sovereign states inter se. Municipal law is the law of nation or country Whereas international law is concerned with external relations, national law deals with domestic affairs. If municipal law regulates the behaviour of individuals, international law regulates that of states. Whereas municipal law is the law of sovereign over individual subjects, international law is not law above but between states. Further, since international law has no legislature, executive or court, with compulsory jurisdiction, it is relatively weaker than municipal law.

The process of interaction between municipal law and international law draws a sharp focus on certain practical problems of great complexity; How far municipal courts are bound by international law? How far treaty obligations are binding on them? Are the national officials bound to execute international obligations even though contrary to state law? What happens when there is a conflict between international law and municipal law? A solution of these problems necessitates a study of juristic theories and the practice of states.

JURISTIC THEORIES

There are four juristic theories regarding the relationship between municipal law and international law.

1. Moinstic Theory

This theory views municipal law and international law as two aspects of the same system of law operating essentially with the same subjects, sources and rules. The monistic theory gained prominence after the First World War. The monistic school finds its most direct antecedents in Durkheim and Duguit. Its recent expositors are Krabbe, Kelsen, Kunz, Scelle and Quincy Wright, etc. According to this theory both municipal law and international law are essentially the same. Both are two branches of the science of law and therefore parts of the same legal system. They are the two phases of one and the same thing. The theory contends that the subjects of the two systems of law are essentially the same. For instance, according to Duguit, subjects of international law are not states but individual members of states. Similarly, Kelson also observes that international law, like all law, is a regulation of human conduct and it is men to whom international law entrusts the responsibility for order. The monists also maintain that the origin and source of the two are the same. To them, both have their origin in a higher law founded on the principles of right and wrong or natural justice. To quote Kelson, "all law except the first has its source in a higher law." It is fallacious to say that consent is the basis of treaty law. Treaties consented to are binding because of legal principle of international law known as Pacta Sunt Servanda, which was itself created through custom. A state, to them, is a legal entity with rights and obligations under international law. Thus to monists, both are of the same fundamental nature, arise from the same unity of the science of law, being manifestions of a single conception of law.

Criticism of monistic theory. The monistic position is generally logical. All the same, we can't altogether ignore some points of difference between the two legal orders. For instance, though a treaty may allow foreigners to purchase land and own properties with a provision that the same would not be expropriated, a national legislation can overvide the provision of non-expropriation. Again, there is a lot of difference between the sanctions of the two systems of law. The sanctions of international law are reprisals and war and not execution or individual punishment as under municipal law. Further, the sphere of validity of international law are unlimited both in duration and in area as compared to municipal law. But the traditional view that international law is valid for states as juristic persons only and not for individual human beings is on more acceptable. To conclude, the two legal orders differ only in degree, not in essence. Although international law is a relatively decentralized coercive order, but here too international organs such as international tribunals and international executive agencies are being established. Whatever difference that exists between the two orders is being narrowed down.

2. Dualistic Theory

This theory has been advocated by Triepel (German) and Anzilotti (Italian). Oppenheim also at times leans to it.[1] It differentiates between the two legal orders. According to this theory international law and municipal law are two distinct systems, with distinguishable subjects and judicial origins. It maintains that both the systems are separate and self contained. "The two are separate bodies of legal norms, emerging in part from different sources, comprising different subjects and having application to different objects." Dualists point out to the following differences between the two legal systems.

(1) The sources of municipal law are statutes and customs grown within boundaries of the state, while the sources of international law are customs grown up within the family of nations and law making treaties. (2) Wheras international law mainly regulates relations between member states municipal law regulates that of individuals. Hence the subjects of the two are not the same. (3) There is also difference with regard to substance of law. Municipal law is sovereign over individuals, but their is no central executive authority to compel observance of the norms of international law.

Criticism of dualistic theory. Regarding the difference of subject it is argued that individuals are gradually becoming subjects of international law. They are acquiring rights in their own capacity along with individual responsibility. Anzilotti says that municipal law is conditioned by the principle that State legislation is obligatory, while international law is conditioned by voluntary agreements between states. But this difference is nullified by the fact that treaties are not less obligatory. Regarding the difference in their source, the critics observe that both the systems ultimately originals from a higher law—the principle of natural justice. To illustrate, equality of individuals and equality of States have the same source. Similarly the principle of self defence is acceptable in both the systems. As a matter of fact, both the systems are complementary rather than contradictory, only their spheres of operation are different.

Starke makes reference to two other theories regarding the relationship between the two systems: (*i*) the Transformation Theory and (*ii*) the Delegation Theory.[2]

3. Transformation Theory

This theory maintains that international legal order is different from municipal legal order. To illustrate, Starke observes that a treaty becomes valid only when it is transformed into the law of a country. He means to say that in order to be applicable it must undergo a process of specific adoption or specific incorporation into municipal law. According to Transformation Theory, there is a difference between treaties which are of the natural of promises and state law which are commands. In English law, an extradition treaty becomes meaningful when the Extradition Act confirms it. That is, in English law there is no power to surrender fugitive criminals is in extradition proceedings to a foreign country without express statutory authority.

This theory suffers from certain fallacies:

(1) Its premise that the two laws are two distinct systems is unacceptable. (2) That international law binds states only is no longer correct. (3) That it requires the transformation of treaties into national law for their enforcement. This practice is not uniform. Some treaties are self operating. If certain treaties require legislative action, it cannot be termed 'transformation'; it is nothing but implementation.

4. **Delegation Theory**

It takes the view that international law constitutes a sort of general constitution which delegates each state the right to decide and determine for itself when a treaty is to come into force and in what manner it is embodied in state law. There is no need of transformation of a treaty. The act is merely an extension of one single act.

This theory is incomplete for it does not satisfactorily meet the main argument of the transformation theory. It assumes the primacy of international order but fails to explain the relations existing between the two systems, for at times national legal order may not yield before international rules or agreement.

To conclude, each of these theories suffers from certain drawbacks. If the dualists have overlooked the increasing importance of modern times of individuals and international organisations as ultimate subjects of International law, the followers of Monism fail to recognise the continuing validity of state sovereignty ascribing primacy to municipal law. Likewise the Transformation Theory loses sight of the distinction that exists between implementation and transformation, for a state only implements the rules of international law when it passes laws for its subjects in conformity with the terms of international treaty or custom. It is difficult to say this theory best reflects the real relationship between the two legal orders. Now let us examine the reaction of national systems, to the application of international law as found in practice.

Practice of States with Regard to Application of International Law in Municipal Sphere

Great Britain. The British practice draws a distinction between customary law and treaties with regard to their operation. The former is a part of the law of the land. To quote Blackston, "the law of nations is here adopted in its full extent by the Common law and is held to be a part of the law of the land." In the well known case of 'Zamora', Lord Parkar observed that "it was the primary duty and function of a Prize Court in England to administer international law." Prize Court are not bound by an order-in-council contrary to international law. The traditional view was affirmed in Western Central Gold Mining Co. Ltd. *vs.* King in which Lord Alverstow observed: "whatever had received the common consent of civilized nations must have received the assent of our country. "But in Chung Chi Cheung *vs.* King Lord Atkin maintained: "International law has no validity in British Courts unless its principles were excepted and adopted by the British Law." Thus British Courts will accept the rules of nternational law only if they are not inconsistent with the statute law of Britain.

With regard to treaties it is recognised that they must receive parliamentary assent for their enforcement. That is, they do not automatically become part of English law unless expressively assented to by the legislature. Britain applies the doctrine of incorporation. This doctrine is based on the principle that a customary principle of international law or a treaty earns recognition in so far as it is accepted as a part of municipal law.

America. The USA has unambiguously applied the doctrine that international law is part of the law of the land. There is presumption in case of conflict that the US Congress did not intend to overrule international law. Unlike Britain the US Constitution gives supreme importance to treaties in Article VI. It provides that "all treaties made under the authority of the US shall be the supreme law of the land." As soon as the Senate ratifies a treaty, it is transformed into American law. As such in case of conflict a treaty will prevail over a Statute provided there is no conflict with the US Constitution. With regard to customary law the US position is akin to British practice. To illustrate, in Pacquet Habana and Lola, Justice Gray observed, "International law is part of our law, and the Prize Courts administring the law of nations were bound to take judicial notice of international law and give effect to it in the absence of any treaty or other public acts of their Government." Accordingly, in this case the Spanish fishing boats were exempted from capture during blockade as per international custom. But in another case, 'Over the Top' (1925), the District Court observed that "international practice is law only in so far as we adopt it, and like all law, it bends to the will of the Congress." This judgement implies that American municipal law making provisions in violation of the principles of international law are binding on American courts, such principles of international law notwithstanding. It means that customary rules of international law as well treaties can be invalidated by subsequent legislation. A treaty is superior to American municipal law only if it is not in conflict with the constitutional law. Besides, the American Courts have drawn a distinction between self-executing and non-self-executing treaties. The former if not inconsistent with the constitution become operative as part of municipal law after ratification. But in the case of non-self-executing treaties requiring legislations, they do not become operative until necessary legislation is passed by the Congress. Thus the American practice is more or less similar to that of Britain.

The doctrine of incorporation though first formulated as an Anglo-American doctrine has received the approval of Courts in France, Belgium, Switzerland and other continental countries. Most of European and Latin American States in their constitution give a broad recognition to the doctrine that the obligations of international law must be transformed into muncipal obligations.

India. The authority for the application of international law is found in Article 51 (Chapter IV) of the Indian Constitution. It provides that the state shall endeavour to foster respect for international law and treaty obligations in the dealings of the organised peoples with one another." Thus our constitution ensures to give high regard to international law and morality. Yet unlike the USA, it has not made treaties the Supreme law of the land. Article 253 of the Indian Constitution empowers Parliament to enact legislation for implementation of treaties. However, legislation is not a mandatory requirement for all treaties.

Soviet Union The Soviet views, however, repudiates the subbordination of internal law to international law. In other words, they reject the supremacy of international law. They have supported a theory which would presuppose throughout the tight dialectic interdependence of the two systems.[3] The Monistic theory is altogether foreign to Communist States.

The practice of other states reveal a wide variety of attitude of municipal courts. By end large, customary rules of international law are applied as part of municipal law in most states without the necessity of any specific act of incorporation, provided there is no conflict with the existing municipal law. Both the International

Courts also maintained that in case of conflicts international law prevalied over municipal law. In other words, municipal law contrary to international law or treaty cannot be pleaded before the world Court. "That municipal law provisions can't prevail over those of treaty" was upheld in the "Greco-Bulgarian Communities" case as well as in "Treatment of Polish nationals in Danzig" case. Clyde Eagleton also maintains that "to admit that municipal law can override international law is to deny the letter." Art. 27 of the Vienna Convention on the Law of Treaties States "A party cannot invoke the provisions of its internal law as justification for its failure to carry out treaty."

Examing the practice of various states, Fenwick observed: (1) as a general principle international law takes priority over municipal law; (2) it is assumed that a treaty signed and ratified is in accord with the constitution and becomes part of the law of the land; (3) subsequent legislation in violation of international treaty is invalid; (4) the specific rules of customary international law and the resolutions of international conference have the full force of legal obligation and are not less binding than treaties.

To conclude, the policy adopted by the world community regarding correlation between the two legal systems is designed to serve the twin goals of stability and change. If municipal law serves particular interest, international law serves global interest and only a synthesis of the two can reconcile the claims of sovereignty with the compulsions of interdependence among nations.[4]

REFERENCES

1. OPPENHEIM, *International Law,* op. cit., p. 37.
2. STARKE, *An Introduction to International Law,* op. cit, pp. 82-83
3. SHARMA, SURYA P., 'Municipal Law' in *World Focus,* New Delhi, Monthly, January, 1983, p. 9.
4. Ibid., pp. 9-10.

Chapter 5

Rights and Duties of States

Like individuals, states are also entitled to some basic or fundamental rights with corresponding duties. The fundamental rights of states are conditions inherent in the very nature of states for their self-development, self-expression and self-assertion.

Until about the end of the 19th century, the natural law jurists maintained that membership of the family of nations bestowed upon the member states certain rights which were called the Fundamental Rights of States, and that these Fundamental Rights were essential, absolute, and self-evident. Since the international community consisted of sovereign states the Fundamental Rights were inherent in the very nature of such states.

The Montevideo Convention of Rights and Duties of States adopted in 1933 was the first authoritative declaration by American States on the subject. Subsequently under the U.N. Charter these rights and duties were reaffirmed. The Draft Declaration on Rights and Duties of States prepared by the International Law Commission enumerated 4 Rights and 7 Duties of States.[1] The Four Rights of States are : (*i*) Right to independence and sovereignty; (*ii*) Right to jurisdiction over state territory; (*iii*) Right to equality: and (*iv*) Right to individual and collective self-defence.

1. Right to Self-Defence or Self-Preservation

One of the fundamental rights recognised by the law of nations is the state's right of existence and this has been made a source of all other rights. To quote Wheaton, "it is the foundation of all other rights." It is an inherent as well as legal right. Article 1 of the Draft Declaration on Rights and Duties of states says: "the first concern of a state is undoubtedly the integrity of its personality and its preservation—the most fundamental right for upon this all other rights are dependent."

From the earliest time self-preservation was considered sufficient justification for many acts of a state which violate the rights of other states. Hall was of the view that "in the last resort almost all the duties of states are subordinated to the right of self-preservation." Every nation is free at all times and regardless of treaty provisions to defend its territory from attack. Every violation/in furtherance of the act of self-preservation can be excused in case of necessity. However, as Webster has observed in 'Caroline'; "necessity to be an excuse of self-defence should be instant, overwhelming and leaving to choice of means and no moment for deliberation." Moreover, the action should not be excessive or unreasonable. The well known cases in which the right of self-defence was involved are: the Danish Fleet case (1807), the Caroline case (1837) and the Corfu Channel case (1946).

Article 51 of the Charter while allowing this right restricts it to the case of "an armed attack" and not in anticipation Moreover, this right exists until the Security Council takes action. Thus it is to be noted that Article 51 has changed the character of the right of self-defence. But since the vigilance of the UN is not enough, the best judge of 'necessity' is still the state itself. Therefore, if a state is attacked directly or indirectly or there is reasonable apprehension to such attack, the counter attack is justified, if it is not out of proportion. But the violation of international law is not to be justified if it can be prevented or redressed otherwise.

The great defect of this doctrine of necessity is that it provides a powerful instrument in the hands of an unscrupulous state to violate the independence of smaller states and set the peace at naught. Quite often an act of aggression is pleaded as an act of self-defence by an aggresor. However, in practice the right to existence depends upon its ability to protect itself. The actual enjoyment of this right, therefore, is conditional upon the physical power at the disposal of the individual states.

2. Right to Sovereignty and Independence

The right to independence is a corollary to the right of national existence. The right to sovereignty means freedom of a state from out side control both in domestic and external affairs. The internal independence implies freedom to adopt any constitution, formulate any foreign policy, conclude treaties, make war and peace. The external independence connotes the freedom of a state to conduct or determine its relation with other states. However, the traditional concept of sovereignty and independence has undergone revolutionary changes. The right of independence is now subject to the limitations of international law. A number of treaties, conventions and declarations put severe restriction on it. Consequently sovereignty today means "the residuum of power which a state posesses within the confines laid down by international law."[2] The establishment of the UNO has shifted emphasis from independence to interdependence. The post-

War division of the world into blocks, military alliances and economic groupings have led to further erosion of state's sovereignty and independence.

3. Right to Equality of States

States are equal as international persons in the family of nation. The United Nations Organisation is based on the sovereign equality of all members. Equality here means equality before law or equal protection of law, which means equality of legal status. It implies that all states have the same rights and obligations. According to Oppenheim, this legal equality has four consequences: (*i*) All states have only one vote each irrespective of size, population, power and wealth; (*ii*) Legal equality confers on each states a right to exercise one vote which is of equal weight whether the state is big or small; (*iii*) No state can claim jurisdiction over another state, its Sovereign Head or public ships (The famous cases on this point are 'Mighell *vs.* Sultan of Jahore' and 'Parlément Belge', discussed elsewhere); and (*iv*) Courts of one state cannot question the validity or legality of official acts of another sovereign state. Further, states cannot be sued without their consent to accept the jurisdiction of another state.[3]

But there are exceptions to the principle of equality even in the UNO. For instance, in matters of substance five permanent members of the Security Council are allowed Veto Power. The doctrine of equality has always been championed only by small states. This doctrine sometimes plays a mischievous roll. Small powers often demand equal representation on international bodies with nominal contribution to their upkeep. No wonder that Brierly has observed: "the whole business of equality is a legal paradox."

4. Right to Exclusive Jurisdiction Over State Territory

International law disallows any encroachment by a state on the territory of another state. A state is entitled to develop itself without molestation, of course, subject to treaty right and corresponding right of other states.

5. Right to Respect and Dignity

Heads of States are entitled to respect and dignity while visiting another state. Even his diplomatic agents enjoy such respect in the states where they are accredited.

Duties of States. In International law, as in municipal law, rights involve certain duties. The rights of one state necessarily implies a corresponding duty on the part of other state. The International Law Commission has, therefore, enumerated 7 duties that all states are required to follow. These duties are:

(1) Non intervention in the affairs of another state.
(2) Refraining from fomenting Civil Strife in another country.
(3) Ensuring peaceful conditions internally to keep international peace.
(4) Refraining from resorting to War, using threat or force against the territorial integrity or political independence of another state.
(5) Abiding by customary and conventional international law.
(6) Settling inter-state disputes peacefully.
(7) Allowing respect for human rights and fundamental freedoms, without maintaining any distinction on any ground whatsoever.

Although it is easy to enumerate duties of states, it is very difficult to get them observed in practice. At best they are only standards of conduct that states are enjoined to observe. These rights and duties of state are reitereted in the Declaration on the Principles of International Law concerning Friendly Relations and Cooperation among States as per the General Assembly Resolution No. 2625 passed on 24 December 1970 and also in the Charter of Economic Rights and Duties of States adopted by the General Assembly in 1974. Some of these rights have been also summarised in what is known as *Panchsheel.*

REFERENCES

1. STARKE, *An Introduction to International Law,* op. cit., p. 105.
2. Ibid, p. 106.
3. OPPENHEIM, *International Law,* op. cit., pp. 263-67.

Chapter 6

Recognition

Recognition is one of the most 'chaotic' subjects—in international law. P.C. Jessup observes that "recognition of a state is the act by which another state acknowledges that the political entity recognised possesses the attributes of statehood."[1] Oppenheim says that "recognisation is a declaration on the part of the recognising state that a foreign community or authority is in possession of necessary qualifications of statehood, of governmental capacity, or of belligerency. Recognition is of many kinds. It may be of new states, new governments, new heads and new territory and also of belligerency.

THEORIES OF RECOGNITION

There are two divergent theories on the subject:

1. Constitutive Theory

According to this theory, recognition is the process by which a political community acquires personality international law by becoming a member of the family of nations. Hegal was the founder of this School. Advocating this theory Oppenheim comments that "a State is and becomes an international person through recognition only and exclusively."[2] Prof. Lauterpacht also supports the constitutive view. Holland too leams to it. He observes that a state cannot be said to have attained maturity unless it is stamped with the Seal of recognition which is indispensable to the full enjoyment of right which it connotes. Poland and Czechoslovakia became international persons through the treaty of Versailles which was a sort of collective recognition. So is the case with Israel as well.

Criticism of constitutive theory. First, to say that unrecognised state has neither rights nor duties at international law is absurd. Secondly, non-recognition of a state by others is not conclusive evidence of the absence of qualifications requisite for statehood. Thirdly, it does not afford the protection of international law to new states until recongnized and hence leaves them to be at large without responsibility. Fourthly, this theory subjects a new state to the superiority of an existing state. Fifthly, a unilateral act of recognition produces legal effects on the recognised entity. Does it not create a lot of confusion when others fail to do so, for it has legal personality for some states only and not for others. Sixthly, this theory gives life to a state which is dependent on the mercy of the existing ones. Lastly, why in case of civil war a belligerent community is accorded a special status as an international person and its prize court's decrees accepted when recognition to the existing state is withheld by some countries?

2. Declaratory or Evidentiary Theory

According to this theory, "the act of recognition is merely a formal acknowledgement of an already established fact." In other words, recognition merely supplies the necessary evidence for this fact. In support of this theory Article 3 of Montivedio Convention (1933) states "the political existence of a state is independent of recognition by other states." The chief exponents of this theory are Hall, Wagner, Fischer, Cobbet, Brierly, etc. To quote Hall, "the state which is theoretically a politically organised community enters as of right into the family of states." The advocates of this theory therefore maintain that recognition should not be withheld if a state shows marks of statehood —permanent population, a defined territory, a well established government and capacity to fulfil international obligations. No wonder Napoleon once remarked: "the French Republic no more needs recognition than the sun requires to be recognised." It means that statehood exists even prior to recognition. To illustrate, the UN Officers conducted cease fire negotiations with people's Republic of China on the Korean issue though most of the states had not recognised it. The state is supposed to come into existence, according to courts, when requirements were fulfilled and not when it is recognised. For example, in Wulfsohn *vs*. Russian Socialist Federated Soviet Republic, the US Court of Appeal held: "the political existence of a State is independent of recognition by other States." The court in this case allowed jurisdictional immunity to RSFSR Government although the US had not recognised it. Similarly, the German-Polish Arbitral Tribunal (1929) also held that recognition is declaratory.

Criticism of declaratory theory. First, if rights and duties are concommitant with defecto existence, why should the grant of recognition and the creation of diplomatic relations also be not an incidental, for deplomatic relationship is assential for the protection of rights and trades. Secondly, if recognition is only a formality and without any significance, then why new states and governments, eagerly seek recognition from others.

All said and done, truth lies somewhere in between the two views.

The correct view is that recognition is both declaratory and constitutive. In fact, recognition is constitutive in nature but declaratory of the existing fact. In the opinion of Prof. Lauterpacht, the constitutive theory is more in practice than the declaratory theory, although the bulk of international practice supports the evidentiary theory. However, Lauterpacht is on a strong wicket when he says that "the unfettered will of the recognising state as the determining factor has played more important part in cases of recognition." At the same time he adds that it is a legal duty to recognise if requirements are fulfilled by a state. But how to enforce this legal duty is the crux of the problem, as Starke has pointed out.[3] He cites examples of Israel and China in particular, as they were not recognised by several countries for years together. All told, there is no rigid rule of international law regarding recognition. As commented by Starke, "the subject of recognition can be presented less as a collection of clearly defined rules or principles than as a body of fluid, inconsistent and unsystematic state practice."[4]

PRINCIPLES OF RECOGNITION

It is a rule of International Law that no new state has a right as against other states to be recognised by them, that no state has a duty to recognised a new state and that a new state before its recoginition cannot claim any right allowed to members of the family of nations. What the function of recognition would be if the mere claim of a community to be an independent state would give it a right to membership of the family of nations in international law. Granting of recognition is unquestionably within the discretion of a state but it should not become a matter of arbitrary will. As a matter of fact recognition belongs more to politics than to law. It is everywhere treated as a matter of policy. That "recognition is facultative and not an obligatory act" is more correct.[5] The general practice shows that recognition is still regarded as essentially a political decision. It is often granted or withheld at Will. Cobbet has aptly remarked: "it is a counter in the harsh game of international politics." Cases are not wanting when Governments-in-exile have been given recognition just for the sake of political advantage, such as propping up a regime of particular persuasion. To sum up, T.C. Chen has observed: "In the last analysis, the question of international recognition is but a reflection of the fundamental cleavage between those who regard the state as the ultimate source of international rights and duties and those who regard it as being under a system of law which determines its rights and duties under that law."

Methods of Recognition

Recognition may be express or implied. The latter is effected through acts which imply an intention to grant recognition. The formal method of recognition however are: (*i*) by entering into a treaty; (*ii*) by admitting to the membership of the UN; (*iii*) by exchanging diplomates; (*iv*) by declaration, unilateral or collective; (*v*) by admitting to an International Conference; and (*vi*) by the formal appointment of its consul.

Recognition of Government

The recognition of a new Government or Head of State is more complex than that of a new state. Such problem arises when a change in the Government is brought about by revolutionary means, that is, by the over throw of the existing Government or when a legal Government is challenged by a new political authority within a state. In the latter case the problem of de facto and de jure recognition crops up. In such cases two tests are applied—the objective test and the subjective test. The objective test is whether the new Government is in effective control of the state without substantial opposition and the subjective test is whether the new Government is prepared to carry out international obligations. The British Practice puts three conditions for giving de facto recognition. They are: (*i*) reasonable assurance and permanence; (*ii*) the government commands popular support; and (*iii*) the government fulfils international obligations.[6] In case of Britain, however, de facto recognition shall prevail over de jure recognition if their claims come into conflict. To illustrate, during the Spanish Civil War (1936-38) the British Government gave de facto recognition to belligerent led by General Franco. His Government was held to be a sovereign state and as such entitled to immunity.

De facto recognition is, however, provisional in nature. Being tentative in character it can be easily withdrawn. De jure means that according to the recognising states the Government recognised formally fulfills the requirement laid down by international law for effective participation in international community. De jure recognition is therefore complete implying full and normal diplomatic relations. It is considered to be retroactive in effect and validates all the actions and conduct of the government so recognised from the commencement of its existence. In Guarantee Trust Co. of Newyork *vs.* USA, it was held that "the recognition of the Soviet Government (1933) left unaffected those legal consequences of the previous recognition of the

Provisional Government and its previous representatives which attached to action taken here prior to later recognition."

Recognition of Belligerency

Recognition of belligerency implies the existence of an organised political group de facto in control of certain territory. It confers an international status on the belligerents for the purposes of War. However, four conditions have to be satisfied before granting the status of belligerency. One, when operation has reached the dimension of an actual war. Two, the rebels are following rules of warfare. Third, other states cannot keep aloof from their operation. Four, belligerents have succeeded in keeping a part of the country in their hand. Such recognition enables the belligerent community and the parent state the same international status with respect to the prosecution of war. The recognition of belligerency includes the belligerent acts of the revolutionaries on the High Seas and in the airspace above.

Recognition of Insurgency

The tests for such recognition are: one, the insurgents have control over a considerable portion of territory; two, they have considerable support from the majority; three, they are willing to carry out international obligations. But it confers no belligerent right such as blockade. Sometimes such recognitions proves premature and precipitous.

INDIAN POLICY OF RECOGNITION

The Government of India has been of the view that tests laid down by the Vienna Convention on Diplomatic Relations (1961) should be followed in matters of Diplomatic Recognition, i.e., such recognition can be given only to the government of a state exercising effective authority within defined geographical limits. From Nehru's time, New Delhi has followed a policy of avoiding de jure recognition of emigre goverments or liberation movements. But in the post-Nehru period New Delhi made an exception in the case of the provisional government established by the Bangladesh Liberation Movement by giving it premature recognition on 6 December 1971. Again, in 1 April 1975 when Indian Government recognised the Peking-based Government-in-exile headed by Prince Sihnouk it made a second exception. However, Indian action in allowing the Palistine Liberation Organisation to set up an office in New Delhi did not amount to de jure recognition until March 1980 when the PLO was given full diplomatic recognition. Apart from this on 7 July 1980 India recognised Heng Samrin regime of Kampuchea which ousted the Pol Pot regime in 1979. Apparently, it is not in consonance with our established policy of opposing the presence of foreign troups in any country. It is a well known fact that the Samrin regime survives only because of Vietnamese troops about two lakh strong. Obviously, it is not consistent with the principle of recognition as laid down by international law, for a government should be recognised only if it has established its hold over a major part of the country concerned. The present Kampuchean regime does not satisfy this test, as the guerilla forces of the Pol Pot Government and the NLF are actively operating in many parts of the country. The writ of the Samrin Government hardly runs over one-third of the country. Incidentally, a majority of the UN members still accept the legitimacy of the Pol Pot Government, now called the Democratic Coalition (tripartite) headed by Sihnouk.

REFERENCES

1. Jessup, P.C., *A Modern Law of Nations*, New York, Macmillan, 1950, p., 4.
2. Oppenheim, *International Law*, op. cit., p. 125.
3. Starke, *An Introduction to International Law*, op. cit., pp. 45-46.
4. Ibid., p. 140.
5. Ibid., p. 146.
6. Smith, H.A. in M.P. Tandon, *Public International Law*, op. cit., p. 116.

Chapter 7

State Succession

According to Starke and Brierly, the term 'Succession' is a misnomer in international field. It presupposes that the analogies of private law are applicable in the case of States also. To these writers there is no general principle of State succession. In the opinion of Oppenheim, "the practice of States also shows that no general succession takes place according to international law." However, it is not correct to say that no succession whatever takes place, these comments notwithstanding. Certain rights and duties do devolve upon an international person from its predecessor.

Succession implies the substitution of one state for another. To quote Oppenheim, "a succession of international person occurs when one or more international persons take the place of another international person in consequence of certain changes in the latter's condition."[1]

Succession is either universal or partial.

1. Universal Succession

(*i*) It takes place when one state completely absorbes another state by conquest, e.g., South African Republic was absorbed by Great Britain in 1901 and Korea by Japan in 1910.

(*ii*) It also takes place when several states agree to merge into a federal state, e.g., the merger of Egypt with Syria (1958-1961), the paper merger of Iraq with Jordan (1958), the merger of 7 Kingdoms into the United Arab Emirates (1970) and the recent merger of Morocco with Libya (1984).

2. Partial Succession

(*i*) It takes place when another state is established by breaking away from parental state, e.g., America broke away from Britain (1776).

(*ii*) By Cession purchase or conquest, e.g., Cession of California to USA (1874), purchase of Louisiana (1803), Florida (1819), and Alaska (1867) by USA.

(*iii*) By dismemberment, e.g., dismemberment of Czechoslovakia (1938), of India (1947), of Pakistan (1971), etc.

CONSEQUENCES OF STATE SUCCESSION

As regards state succession the practice is not uniform. There is great uncertainty about it. It is on account of this uncertainty of the law of succession that all contingencies arc now covered by treaties between the concerned parties.

Rights and Obligations Arising Out of Succession

1. **Treaty Rights and Obligations.** (*a*) *Succession in political treaties.* It depends upon the nature of succession. If federation is formed, all treaties made by the units prior to its formation are extinguished. If the state is enlarged, by conquest or absorption, old obligations continue. As regards political rights and duties, no succession whatever takes place. That is, all treaties of alliance, neutrality and personal treaties disappear. Even Extradition treaties may expire after succession.

(*b*) *State succession in respect of law making treaties.* As regards law making treaties such as multilateral conventions regarding health, narcotics, rivers and canals, innocent passage, etc., certain writers like Hall, Holland, Oppenheim, Brierly, Wheaton and Fenwick lean in favour of the "clean state" rule. But Westlake, Kent and Field, etc., take a contrary view. To them, treaties of general utility survive. To Prof. Huber, commercial treaties pass over to the succeeding state. McNair sums up that "clean state" is applicable only when there is no political continuity or political dismemberment.

2. **Public property and public rights.** The new state succeeds to all public proprietory rights such as railways, roads and rivers. It can collect taxes that are due to the replaced state. In Polish Upper Silesia case the P.C.I.J. held that state succession to public property of the annexed or ceded territory is the customary principle of international law even in the absence of treaties.

3. **Private property.** Private rights are valid against the succeeding states. They do not cease on a change of sovereignty unless changed by a new constitution or legislation.

4. **Contractual liability.** That an absorbing state is bound by contractual obligation is a recognised rule of international law. However the British view favours termination of concession given by the preceeding state. But the modern view on the other hand favours recognition or continuation of concession. A contractual rights of the nature of a vested right must be respected. The present practice has modified the doctrine of non-succession as laid down by Lord

Alverston in the case of Westrand Central Gold Mining Co. Ltd. *vs.* King. The P.C.I.J. in it's advisory opinion in "German Settlers in Poland" case (1923) supported it. It advised: "A cession of territory does not operate as a cession of the property belonging to its inhebitants." The same view was reitrated in Mavrommatis-Palestine Concession case (1924) wherein the same court maintained that the British Government as mandatory power cannot rescind the concession allowed to the Greek subject by the previous Turkish Government. However, it dismissed the Greek Government's claim for indemnity as Mavrommatis had suffered financial loss.

5. **Public debts.** It depends on the nature of succession. If only one nation succeeds it takes the entire burden of public debt, e.g., Prussia took over debt of German States in (1966). If many states succeed the debt is divided proportionally among the succeeding states. For instance, public debts were divided between Austria and Hungery (1919), between India and Pakistan (1947), between Pakistan and Bangladesh (1971). However, when debts are divided assets are also proportionally shared. The division of public debt between Pakistan and Bangladesh is still awaiting solution. Bangladesh demands 56% share of the assets without liability. She is not willing to share £ 1,600 million public debt. Her argument is that she had contributed 40% of the Central budget. Jute alone represented 40% export and trade earnings. Again, East Pakistan contributed anywhere between 50-60% of the total foreign exchange but its share of total imports was less than 35% only. But it is to be noted that only that part of public debt passes over to the successor which does not pertain to war purposes.

6. **Torts.** A conquerer successor is not liable for the torts of the government displaced. As regards the unliquidated damages for torts, the succeeding state is not liable. To illustrate, Robert Brown's (US Citizen) claim was not accepted by the Arbitration Tribunal against the South African Republic (1923) to which the British Government was the successor.

7. **Membership of International Organisations.** The membership of such organisations does not pass over to successors automatically. Hence when India was divided (1947), the membership of all international organisations solely devolved on India and not Pakistan. Pakistan had to be admitted afresh on 30 September 1947. Similarly, when the United Arab Republic was founded (1958) as a result of merger between Syria and Egypt, Syria lost her membership of the UNO. However, Syria again became a member of the United Nations when she broke away from the UAR in 1961.

8. **International Organisations.** The United Nations replaced the League of Nations in 1945. So did the International Court of justice, which succeeded the Permanent Court of International Justice. Similarly, International Civil Aviation Organisation replaced International Commission for Air Navigation; the World Health Organisation replaced International Sanitary Bureau. But on the question of South-West Africa (Namibia) the World Court rejected (1950) the UN claim to bring it into the Trusteeship System. It held that UN succeeded only to the supervisory functions of the League of Nations and the Mandatory claim of the Union of South Africa still exists.[2] But since the South African Government failed to fulfil its mandatory obligations, the World Court in its advisory verdict (1971) considered South Africa's presence in South-West Africa to be illegal,[3] and upheld the termination of its mandate which had already been resolved by the UN General Assembly (1964).

9. **Laws.** The civil law continues unless changed after the succession. But the public law changes with the transfer of sovereignty.

10. **Nationality.** Previously the old nationality was lost on a change of sovereignty. But now the citizens are allowed option to choose nationality within a prescribed period.

REFERENCES

1. OPPENHEIM, *International Law*, op. cit., p. 157.
2. I.C.J. Reports (1950), p. 79.
3. TANDON, M.P., *Public International Law*, op. cit., p. 139.

Chapter 8

State Territory

One of the essential elements of statehood is the occupation of a defined territory. The territory of a state is that definite portion of the surface of the globe with well defined boundaries which is subjected to the sovereignty of a state. In other words, "it is that portion of the earth's surface over which a state exercises supreme and exclusive sovereignty."[1] According to Swarclien, "the territory of a State is composed of all the land, water surface within its boundaries and jurisdiction, all the earth and water below the surface and the air above it."[1] That is, it comprises land territory, territorial waters, national waters, and air-space over and sub-soil underneath.

LIMITATIONS ON TERRITORIAL SOVEREIGNTY

Ordinariy, a territory is under exclusive control of a state, but exceptions are also there, e.g., in case of condominium the sovereignty is shared by two states. Again, sovereignty may be restricted under military pacts as well. Hence the traditional concept of unrestricted sovereigntly is no more feasible.

Boundaries

A state territory is determined by its borders. Oppenheim definds boundaries "as the lines separating the territory of one State from that of another or from unappropriated territory or from the High Seas." According to Jones, "a boundary is not merely a line but a line in a border land."[2] Boundary may or may not be a barrier. It may be natural or artificial. Natural boundaries are formed by rivers, seas, hills, deserts or forests. Artificial boundary may consists of walls, poles, pillars, barbed wired and roads, etc. To give examples, half of boundary like between USA and Canada is artificial along 19th parallel. Similarly, Vietnam was divided on 17th parallel during (1954-75), Korea is divided on 38th parallel since 1948. Certain well-known international boundaries are the MacMahon Line between India and Tibet, Durand Line between Pakistan and Afganistan. Great difficulty however arises in water boundary. In non-navigable river, it runs down in the middle. But if it is navigable, it runs through the Thalweg of the river—the middle of the deepest navigable channel. The advantage of Thalweg is that the boundary line follows more closely the thoroughfare of commerce and less subject to change. In the case of New "Jersy *vs.* Delaware" decides in 1934, the US Supreme Court upheld the principles of dividing the river boundaries by the middle of the main channel—the median line. The Thalweg principle is applicable to bays as well. Boundary disputes are solved by negotiation, arbitrations and conventions.

Rivers

Rivers are part of the territory of riparian states. Some rivers are national rivers such as Thames where foreigners have seek permission for navigation. But some rivers are international rivers owned by several states who can regulated navigation in their respective portions. Again, some rivers are internationalized by treaties. Further, some rivers are boundary rivers, e.g., rainy river between the USA and Canada. If a river divides two states, the boundary shifts with the course of the river. Amongst the most prominent river disputes are the Indus River dispute between India and Pakistan, which was happily settled in 1960, the Jordan River dispute between Israel and Jordan, the Shaat-al-Arab dispute between Iraq and Iran, the Ussuri River dispute between China and the Soviet Union, the Ganga River dispute between India and Bangladesh, etc.

Rivers as international waterways. The flow of an international river is not within the arbitrary power of one of the riparian states. It can't be directed to the disadvantage of others. In 1815, several rivers like Rhine and Elbe were opened to all nations. By the Treaty of Paris (1856), Danube was internationalized and a Commission was appointed to regulate its navigation. The Peace Treaty of 1919 declared many rivers open to all rivers such as Oder, Vistula, etc. The Paris Peace Conference (1947), reiterated that Danube shall remain free and open to all.

Principal Rivers

1. **Rhine River.** The Rhine River was first internationalized by the Treaty of Paris (1815). The Congress of Vienna (1815), the convention of Mannheim (1868) and the Versailles Treaty (1919) reiterated that its navigation shall be free and open to all. In 1936 Germany denounced the provision regarding the International Commission established in 1868. However, it was reopened to navigation after the Second World War.

2. **Danube River.** The Danube River is 1725 miles long flowing

from Germany via Austria, Hungary, Romania, Yugoslavia leading to Black Sea. For a long time the navigation of lower Danube was reserved to Russia and Turkey. But under the Treaty of Paris (1856) this monopoly was abolished. It was placed under the supervision of European Danube Commission. The Berlin Treaty of 1878 further enlarged and enhanced the power of this Commission. The 12 powers interested in the Danube River declared it free for navigation in 1921. The Paris Peace Conference (1947) declared that it shall remain open to all.

3. **Congo River.** The Congo River is the largest river in Africa. The Convention of 1884 recognised Portugal's sovereignty over it, as it was she who had first discovered Congo. But at the Berlin Conference of 1885, it was declared free. The Berlin Convention was reconsidered by the Convention of St. Germain (1919) when the signatories declared to maintain a complete commercial equality.

Principal Canals

Canals are artificially constructed and therefore part of the state. But when a canal connects to open seas they are often neutralised or internationalised. The three well known interoceanic canals are: (1) Suez Canal, (2) Kiel Canal, (3) Panama Canal.

1. **Suez Canal.** The Suez Canal is the most important of the inter-oceanic canals. It is 103 miles (150 km) long connecting the Mediterranean Sea to the Red Sea. It was owned by a French company but the controlling interest was held by Britain. It came under the British Control in 1883 when Egypt became a British protectorate. The Charter of the Canal was to expire on November 17, 1969 and thereafter the canal was to be the property of Egypt. The Canal was to remain open at all times to merchant men and men of war of all nations as per the convention of Constantinople, which was signed by 9 countries in 1888. The Canal has been guarded by the British garrison as it has been a life line of the British Empire. According to Anglo-Egyptian Treaty of 1936 the canal came to be regarded as an integral part of Egypt but Britain was allowed to station troops untill 1956. In 1950, King Farouk of Egypt demanded cancellation of the 1936 Treaty. After long negotiation the British troops were to be evacuated by an agreement of 1954. The whole of 8,000 strong garrison was to leave by June 20, 1956. This agreement recognised the canal as part of Egypt, and as a waterway of international importance.

Having been rebuffed by the US and UK for military and economic assistance, President Nasser, the ruler of Egypt, announced nationalization of the Canal in 1956 and freezed the Company funds in Egypt. On the protest of France and Britain a 24-nation Conference was called in London. Nasser rejected the decision of this Conference. Then the dispute was referred to the Security Council which affirmed 6 principles. But the plan for International Control as moved by the Council was vetoed by the Soviet Union. Then came the 'stupid' and 'disastrous' attack by Israel supported by Anglo-French forces on October 29, 1956. However, a ceasefire was brought about with the UN efforts. Ultimately, in 1957, Egypt under took to respect the 1888 convention and agreed to refer any complaint against the Canal Administration and deposited its acceptance of compulsory jurisdication of the I.C.J. The World Bank announced in 1958 that an agreement had reached regarding settlement of compensation to shareholders and final agreement was signed at Geneva on 13 July 1958. On June 6, 1967 Egypt announced that Suez Canal shall remain closed to traffic indefinitely as a sequel to war with Israel (1956). The canal could be reopened only on 5 June 1975.

2. **Kiel Canal**. The Kiel Canal was constructed in 1896 by Germany. It connects North Sea to the Black Sea, and runs wholly through Germany. It also joins the Baltic Sea with the North Atlantic Ocean. Before the First World War Germany could close it at will. But the Versailles Treaty provided that "it shall remain open to the vessels of Commerce and War of all nations at peace with Germrny on terms of entire equality."

In 1921, a British Vessel (S.S. Wimbledon) chartered by a French Company was refused access on the charge that it was carrying military material to Poland who was at war with the Soviet Union. But the P.C.I.J. held Germany guilty under Article 380 of the Versailles Treaty. Germany could not advance her neutrality orders against the obligation requiring Keil to remain opened to state at peace with Germany even if there was a war between two states in which Germany was neutral. In 1936, Germany again denounced this article and required foreign naval crafts to obtain permission of entry. But after the Second World War its obligation was revived.

3. **Panama Canal**. The Panama Canal was constructed by the USA, over a period of 14 years. It was opened in August 1914. It is 80 km long and connects the Pacific Ocean with the Atlantic Ocean. Its international status was governed by the Hay-Pauncefote Treaty between Britain and the USA (1903). The canal maintained its neutralized character subject to the right of the US under the terms of 1903 Treaty (amended in 1936). The US could fortify and use it as a military base. She guaranteed Panama her independence in lieu of

the grant in perpetuity of land five miles on either side of the canal. As sole guarantor of neutrality she could close it in war. On the outbreak of the First World War, the US regulated the passage of belligerent warships and prizes. When the US herself became a belligerent (1916), a proclamation excluded all enemy vessels save with the consent of the canal authorities. The same line was adopted during the Second World War too. On January 14, 1942 the President Roosevelt issued a proclamation declaring the Gulf of Panama a "Maritime Control Area" for purposes of defence and the protection of approaches to it.

Since 1963-64 Panama had been demanding full sovereignty over the canal. After 14 years of negotiation a tentative agreement on Panama Canal was negotiated. Under this agreement (1977) the US would transfer full control of the canal to the Republic of Panama by A.D. 2000 and phase down its basis from 14 to 3. Although it makes a distinct difference from the old position, yet even under this agreement the US retains the right to interfere in case the canal and its passage is endangered.

Straits

A strait is "a narrow passage connecting two sections of the High Seas." There are about 116 straits in the world. Some of the well known straits are Dover, Gibralter, Harmouz and Malacca. All straits not wider than 6 miles are territorial in international law. Certain straits are subject to special local regulations. In the Corfu Channel case the World Court observed: "In times of Peace warships are allowed passage without the previous authorization of a coastal State, provided the passage is innocent."[3] But the new Sea Law Treaty (1982) provides for a nonsuspendable transit passage through straits which are used for international navigation. It states: "in straits all ships and aircrafts enjoy right of transit passage which shall not be impeded. Nevertheless, it has accommodated the concern of strait states with respect to their security, safety, pollution, including the right to designate sea lanes.

Dardanelles and Bosphorus. They connect the Mediterrenean Sea with the Black Sea and belong to Turkey. Till 1841 it was under full Turkish control. Later on Turkey controlled it subject to neutralization rules till the 19th century. After 1918 it was opened to all and placed under International Commission. After the victory of Kamal's Turkey over Greece a Convention was signed at Lausanne (1923) whereby signatories declared both the straits open to all. It mitigated International Control by partly restoring Turkish Sovereignty. Subsequently, the Montreux Convention of 1936 revived her full sovereignty subject to certain conditions. It provided for remilitarization and refortification. International Commission was also abolished. The Montreux Convention still lasts. Although at the Potsdam Conference (1945) Great Powers agreed to revise it but serious differences arose over the terms of revision between the Soviet Union and the US supported by Britain. In 1946 the Soviet Union proposed to keep the Straits free to merchant marines of all nations during War and to transit of Black Sea Powers at all times. Its implication was that the warships of non-Black Sea Powers will not be allowed to pass through except with the consent of Black Sea Powers or in the excution of UN action. Naturally, the Soviet proposal was outrightly turned down.

LAW OF THE SEA—JURISDICTION ON THE SEA

The sea occupies merely 70 per cent of the surface of our globe. In other words, about three-fourths of the earth is covered with water. For legal purposes the sea is divided into six zones: (1) Internal Sea; (2) Territorial Sea; (3) Continental Shelf; (4) Contiguous Zone; (5) Exclusive Economic Zone and (6) High Seas.

1. **Internal sea.** It consists of ports, harbours, gulfs, bays, straits, etc. In national waters the coastal state may apply and enforce its laws in full. Foreign states have no rights there except under a treaty.

2. **Territorial sea/maritime belt.** Territorial water is that part of the Sea which is under the sway of the littoral states. Every state is entitled to regard a certain area of the sea adjoining its coast as maritime belt. The coastal state exercises jurisdiction over territorial waters due to necessity of self-defence, enjoyment of fishing rights and other advantages. To quote Colombos, "the term territorial waters is used to indicate that part of the sea which extends from a line parallel to the shore to a specified distance therefrom commonly fixed by the majority of maritime states at 3 nautical miles measured from low water mark." This 3 miles limit has been accepted since the end of the eighteenth century, because at that time the range of artillery (cannon shot) was about 3 miles. Now since the range of coastal batteries during Bynkershoek (Dutch) days was about 3 nautical miles, this fact established a principle according to which the limit of a nations' territorial sea was determined by its defensive capabilities. (But now, given the greater range of artillery, missiles and other weapons (200 miles), the extension of Bynkershoek's

principle to our times would be absured). Lord Stowell had accepted this limit of 3 miles in the famous Anna Case (1805).

This limit was also adopted by an Anglo-American Agreement in 1818 by the British Territorial Jurisdiction Act, and later by the Suez Canal Convention (1888), etc.

However, this customary limit has become unacceptable to several countries. Most of the countries favour 12 miles. Still others go to the extent of 200 miles. In the famous Anglo-Norwegian Fisheries case (1951) the I.C.J. allowed 4 miles territorial water limit drawn from not low water mark (because Norway's coast was not uniform) and upheld the 1935 Order of the Government of Norway. Here it is interesting to note that only 21 out of 86 nations had accepted this customary rule at the First Sea Law Conference of 1958 at Geneva. Now the consensus of opinion is in favour of 12 miles (19 km) and this has been finally adopted by the Third Sea Law Convention (1982).

Regime on the Territorial Sea. Article 1 of Geneva Convention (1958) states that coastal states have sovereignty over it subject to limitation that foreign ships have a right of innocent passage. The Western Powers want to extend this right of innocent passage to warships also but the Communist States don't agree to it. The rights of coastal states over territorial sea are : (*i*) Exclusive right to fish, exploit resources of the sea bed and subsoil, (*ii*) Exclusive enjoyment of airspace: Foreign aircrafts are not allowed passage through territorial waters; (*iii*) They can enact navigation, health and custom rules and duties; (*iv*) They have certain power of arrest over merchant ships; (*v*) Warship cannot pass through it without permission; (*vi*) The coastal state has concurrent jurisdiction over crimes on foreign merchant ships, (*vii*) Jurisdiction over foreign ships. No charges can be levied except for specific services. Coastal states have no criminal jurisdiction over foreign ships except when the interest of coastal states are involved and where assistance is sought, e.g., for the suppression of the narcotic traffic. Regarding Civil Jurisdiction the coastal states can't stop or divert foreign ship but they can arrest them in respect of assumed obligations. These rules apply to public ships used for commercial purposes excluding warships. The coastal states has a limited jurisdiction over foreign ships in its territorial sea in respect of matters like revenue, police and sanitation; (*viii*) No state can commit acts within territorial sea so as to violate its sovereignty. If a foreign state commits an offence in territorial waters, the coastal state has a right of pursuing it up to the High Seas under the doctrine of "hot pursuit".

3. **Continental Shelf.** Untill 1945 there was no exclusive right to any part of the sea-bed or subsoil of the High Seas. It was President Truman (US) who first enunciated the doctrine of continental shelf through his proclamations of September 1945. The doctrine was concerned with the urgency of conserving and utilizing the natural resources on the Sea-bed of the High Seas at a particular depth (200 metres or 600 feet). The Truman proclamation claimed the right of jurisdiction, protection and control over continental shelf including the water covering this shelf to a depth of 200 metres at low side. Following the USA, other countries such as Mexico, Argentina, Chile, Peru, Costa Rica, etc., also claimed a similar right.

The International Law Commission defined it "as that part of the sea-bed contiguous but outside the area of marginal seas where the depth of the superjacent waters admitted of the exploitation of natural resources of the sea-bed and and subsoil." The term continental shelf has been defined at the UN Conference on the Law of the Sea (1958) to extend to the outer edge of the continental margin. As per Article I of Geneva Convention (1958) the terms refers (*a*) to the sea-bed and subsoil of the submarine area adjacent to the coast but outside the area of the territorial sea, to a depth of 200 metres or beyond that limit to where the depth of the superjacent water admits of the exploitation of the natural resources of the said area, (*b*) to the sea-bed and subsoil of similar submarine areas adjacent to the coast of island." The continental shelf is by definition an area physically extending the territory of most coastal states into a spacious submerged platform.

The legal source of right here is derived from the land. The Principle applied here is that the land dominates the sea. The continental shelf therefore is the natural prolongation of the coastal state. According to the Third Sea Law Convention (1982), continental shelf shall comprise the sea-bed and the subsoil of the submarine area that extend beyonds its territorial sea throughout the natural prolongation of its land territory to the outer edge of the continental margin or out to a distance of 200 nautical miles from the base lines even if the outer edge of the continental margin is at a lesser distance from the coast. But the fixed point defining the outer limit of the continental shelf shall not exceed 350 nautical miles (560 km) from the coast, or 100 miles from the 2500 metres isobath, whichever is farther seaward.

Jurisdiction Over Continental Shelf. The coastal states have sovereign and exclusive right of exploiting their continental shelf. But this right does not extend in the seas and airspace above; it cannot impede laying submarine cables and pipelines. Further, it should not interfere with navigation, fishing or conservation of the living resources of the sea. The coastal state, however, can operate installations and establish safety zones.

The determination of the continental shelf between adjacent or opposite states shall be effected by agreement in accordance with equitable principles, employing where appropriate, the median or equidistance line and taking account of all the relevant circumstances. In the "North Sea Continental Shelf" case between Germany *vs.* Netherlands and Denmark, the application of equidistance principle as per Article 6 of Geneva Convention of 1958 would have given West Germany only 5 per cent of the sea-bed of the North Sea compared with 10 per cent for Denmark and 11 per cent for Netherlands. This is so because West Germany's North Sea coast has concave shape. That is why she had not ratified Geneva Convention of 1958. The World Court held that the equidistance method of delimitation as laid down by Article 6 of the Geneva Convention does not bind the Federal Republic of Germany. West Germany stood for the principle of equitable apportionment and the same was accepted by the Court. The Court rejected the Dutch-Danish argument that the equidistance principle had become a part of the customary international law.[4]

4. **Contiguous zone**. Article 24 of the Geneva Convention of the Law of the Sea (1958) states: "On the High Sea adjacent to the marginal Sea, a coastal state may take such measures as may be necessary for the enforcement within its territorial waters or territory of its custom, navigation, sanitary or police laws or regulations for its immediate protection."[5] It is beyond territoritorial waters and forms a part of the Hign Seas. The coastal state therefore cannot excercise sovereignty over it, except exercising traditional rights of fishing. The I.L.C. recognised the contiguous zone and put 12 miles limit for it. T h Geneva Convention of 1958 too recognised this right within 12 miles limit in order to prevent and punish infringement of its sanitary or immigration laws. But now this limit has been extended to 24 nautical miles under the new Sea Law Convention of 1982.

4. **Exclusive economic zone**. The concept of exclusive economic zon e is the most significant result of UNCLOS-III. It is hailed as the most dynamic and important development in the law of the sea. It is an area beyond but adjacent to the territorial sea of a coastal state which may not extend beyond 200 nautical miles (320 km) from the base line from which the breadth of the territorial sea is measured. Within the EEZ, the coastal state

would have sovereign rights for the purpose of exploring and exploiting, conserving and managing the natural resources, whether living or non-living, of the sea-bed and subsoil and the subjacent waters and also with regard to other activities such as production of energy from water currents and winds. It would also have jurisdiction to establish and use artificial is lands, installations and structures, marine scientific research and the preservation of the marine environment. But in the exercise of its rights and performance of duties it is obliged to have due regard to the similar rights of other states. The only two important High Sea freedoms significantly ommitted are the freedom of fishing and freedom of marine scientific research. Further, all states shall generally enjoy the freedom of navigation and overflight and the laying of submarine cable and pipelines within the zone. It is interesting to note that landlocked states (31) have rights to participate on an equitable basis in the exploitation and appropriate part of the surplus of the living resources of these zones, unless a state proves its exclusive dependence of those resources. Besides, resource oriented research would be undertaking only with the consent of other states and only for peaceful purposes.

For the present, as demanded by the several countries, the possibility of the EEZ being assimilated to the status of the territorial sea is clearly excluded, as ownership right of the zone relate to economic resources only, where no proprietory right can be claimed as coastal territory. Nevertheless, it can be said that the EEZ would be eventually serve as an intermediate step facilitating the future recognition of a 200 mile territorial sea.

Indian Maritime Legislation. Even before the Third Convention on the Sea Law could take in final shape, a number of states took steps to pass legislation on the basis of the trend of discussion at several sessions of UNCLOS-III. For instance, Mexico adopted legislation to establish 200 miles EEZ *w.e.f.* June 1976. Similarly, the USA enacted a *Fishing, Conversation* and Management Act, in April, 1976. Canada and Norway too expressed their intention to establish 200 miles fishery zone by 1977. Taking cue from these countries India could not afford to lag behind.

India has about 4,000 miles long coastal line and 1280 is lands. Our maritime jurisdiction has so far been regulated by proclamation issued by the President of India on August 30, 1955, concerning the Continental Shelf, on November 29, 1956, concerning fishery conservation zones and on September 30, 1967, concerning the extension of territorial waters to 12 nautical miles. Bearing in mind the consenses and rends at the Third Sea Law Conference, the Indian Parliament adopted two measures in 1976. By the first a reference to the exclusive economic zone and its resources has been added to Article 297 of our Constitution (40th Amendment). The second measure relates to maritime zones. The maritime zones of India include the territorial waters of 12 nautical miles, the contiguous zone of 24 nautical miles, the continental shelf and the exclusive economic zone both of 200 nautical miles from the nearest point from the base line and the historical waters of India. The lands of India will have the same maritime zones as the mainland. According to Maritime Zone Act of 1976, all lands, minerals and other things of value underlying the territorial waters, or the continental shelf, or the exclusive economic zone, as well as other resources of the exclusive economic zone, vest in the Union to be held for the purposes of the Union. The Act further provides that all foreign ships other than war ships including submarines and under water vehicles shall enjoy the right of innocent passage through the territorial waters. Foreign warships can pass through only after giving prior notice to the Central Government. In relation to the contiguous area, the Central Government can exercise powers and take necessary action with respect to the Security of India, immigration, sanitation, customs and other fiscal measures. Following India other states such as Pakistan, Bangladesh, Sri Lanka, Iceland passed similar legislation for the purpose. It became a sort of contagion thereafter.

6. **High Sea or the Open Sea**. The term open sea implies "the coherent body of salt water, the territorial straits, gulfs and bays which are parts of the Sea." Higgins and Colombos described the High Sea "as so much of the ocean as is exterior to a line running parallel with the shore and some distance therefrom." But the concept of the High Sea has undergone a sea change in the last few years. Today only those parts of the sea that are not included in the territorial sea or internal waters of the state, in the EEZ or in the archipelagic waters of an archipelagic state may rightly be termed high seas.

The high sea is not capable of continuous occupation and not susceptible to permanent appropriation. The vagrant waters of the ocean are thus necessarily free. Again, the high sea is inexhaustible. According to Burgh, "the open sea is common to all nations for the purpose of commerce and as a means of intercourse amongst mankind." Upon the ocean in time of peace all states possess an entire equality. It is the common high way of all and appropriated to the use of all. No wonder the UN General Assembly, at the suggestion of Arvid Pardo (Malta), as its 22nd sessions in 1967 declared the high sea as "common heritage of mankind".

Legal Conception on the Freedom of the High Seas

The freedom of the high seas is now well settled. Its legal position is based on the conception that it is common and open to all. It is not susceptible to national appropriation by claims of sovereignty, exclusive use, and occupation of any other nation.

Freedom of the High Seas

As per Articles 1 and 2 of the Geneva Convention of 1958, freedom of the high seas comprises, interalia, freedom of navigation, freedom of fishing, freedom to lay submarine cables and pipelines and freedom to fly over the high seas. These freedoms, however, should be exercised by all states with due regard to the interest of other states. In no case it should be used for any military purpose.

Jurisdiction on the High Seas

(*i*) Nationality of ships—All ships on the high seas are subject to the jurisdiction of states whose flags they fly. (*ii*) Warships and ships owned by states for non-commercial service enjoy complete immunity on the high seas from the jurisdiction of any state other than the flag state. (*iii*) In times of war, warships have a right to investigate merchantships to ascertain if they are attempting to break blockade, carry contraband or rendering unneutral service. (*iv*) In times of peace a state has the right of search of a merchantship if it is engaged in piracy or in slave trade or flying wrong flag, every state is entitled to arrest and try a pirate. But a seizure of such ships without adequate guards would render the state liable for damages and compensations. That is, a seizure can be carried out only by warships or military aircrafts or other ships authorised by the government. (*v*) Hot Pursuit—"A vessel may be pursued upon the high seas and there seized, if it has committed a violation of law of a foreign state while within its territorial waters. This right is allowed under the doctrine of "hot pursuit."[6] (*vi*) Collision—In case of collision only the flag state or the state whose persons are involved can institute any proceedings against the culprit. This rule, significantly, goes against the decision of S.S. Lotus case (1926), which had allowed concurrent jurisdiction. (*vii*) Navigation on the high seas can be closed on account of atomic experiment. States can also adopt anti-pollution measures and thereby put restrictions on navigation in the interest of safety at sea.

Doctrine of Freedom of the Seas and its Limitations

It is well known that the present structure of the law of the sea was devised after the industrial revolution in Europe and it has been developed according to the needs of the European society during the last three centuries. Obviously, the traditional law of nations is a law of European lineage. The widely accepted doctrine of freedom of the sea was based essentially on the vastness and inappropriability of the ocean and inexhaustibility of their resources but all this has now entirely changed. The high noon of the freedom of the high seas—of *laissez faire* in the ocean—has irrevocably passed. In recent years, the accelerating pace of technological, economic, social and political changes has radically altered man's relation to the sea. Today the right of free navigation affects national security. Again, at present about twenty per cent of the world's oil and natural gas comes from under water wells on the continental shelves. Further, scientists are now looking at tides as new sources of energy. Fishing is no more a cottage industry but a highly merchanised and multimillion dollar business. According to one estimate the ocean (beyond EEZ) contains four billion tonnes of yearly yield of fish and three trillion tonnes of mineral nodules. The market value of these minerals is estimated to be about three trillion dollors.[7] Consequently, freedom of the seas now really means unequal freedom or only freedom for the few. It is little wonder that only a few great maritime powers are champions of the freedom of the sea. On the other hand, the small, weak, poor and underdeveloped states are getting deeply concerned about the continued over exploitation of their coastal areas by the big maritime powers. They have seriously started questioning the value of the doctrine of the freedom of seas which, however, useful it might have been in the past, has become outmoded and tyrannical today. They have a feeling that because of this doctrine they are treated as a "second class citizen."[8] They want to treat the high sea as common heritage of mankind.

With the rapidly depleting resources on land and their inadequacy to meet the growing demands for minerals and energy, there is an increasing awareness amongst nations of their urgent need to explore and utilize fully the resources from the oceans. The sea vegetation is supposed to the nine times that of land vegetation. They include both living and non-living matter. The deep ocean floor is endowed with commercially valuable polymetallic nodules. The nodules contain as many as 32 elements of which only 4—manganese, copper, nickel and cobalt—have been proved to be economically and technologically extractable at the moment. No wonder there is a clamour for a new legal order on the ocean.

NEW INTERNATIONAL MARINE ORDER

A new convention on the law of the sea was adopted on April 30, 1982 by UNCLOS-III at its final session (11th) at New York by a vote of 130 states. The Convention comprises some 320 Articles and 9 Annextures.[9] It is designed to establish a new International Marine Order. So as to provide adequate protection to Third World's legitimate interests in the ocean. Almost every conceivable human use of the ocean is covered (25 subjects and issues) by the Convention—navigation and overflight; shipping and fishing; exploration and exploitation of the non-living resources; conservation of the natural resources and protection of the maritime environment; and maritime and scientific research in the multifarious uses of the oceans. It is a guide for states' practice in the oceans of the world, defining maritime zones, laying down rules for drawing maritime boundaries and assigning legal duties and responsibilities and provides also for the settlement of disputes stemming from the multifarious uses of the oceans.

Territorial sea. The coastal state has sovereignty over its territorial sea. It may not be broader than 12 nautical mile (19 km) measured from the appropriate base line based on the low water mark. Foreign shipping vessels are allowed innocent passage through it (passage is deemed innocent if it is not prejudicial to the peace, good order and security of the coastal states).

Straits. In straits used for international navigation, ships and aircrafts of all countries enjoy the right of "transit passage" as long as they proceed without delay and without threatening the bordering states.

Exclusive economic zone. The EEZ is an area beyond but adjacent to the territorial sea of a coastal state, which may not extend beyond 200 nautical miles from the base line from which the breadth of the territorial sea is measured. Within this zone the coastal state has sovereign right over the living and non-living resources of the sea-bed and subsoil and the superjacent waters.[10] The coastal state may adopt appropriate measures to conserve, explore and exploit their natural resources. As regards navigation, other states enjoy traditional freedoms (freedom of navigation, over flight, laying of submarine cables and pipelines) of the high seas. The coastal states rights and obligations in the zone are balanced with the rights of land locked and geographically disadvantages states in the region, both of which have the right to participate, on an equitable basis, in the exploitation of an appropriate part of surplus of living resources of the EEZ.

Continental shelf. The concept and legal regime of the continental shelf (which has its roots in the Truman proclamation of August 1945) has been modified, improved upon and adopted. The continental shelf of a state comprises the sea-bed and subsoil of the submarine areas that extend beyond its territorial sea throughout the natural prolongation of its land territory. The coastal states have sovereign and exclusive rights over the continental shelf to explore it and exploit its natural resources without affecting the legal status of the water or airspace above. The continental shelf would extend to at least 200 nautical miles from the shore and is not to exceed 350 nautical miles (560 km) except under certain specified conditions and circumstances. But they would have to share with the international community a part of the revenue that they may derive from exploiting the oil and mineral resources from any part of their shelf beyond the 200 nautical miles mark.

High seas. While retaining the traditional freedoms of the high seas (freedom of navigation; freedom of fishing; freedom of overflight and freedom of laying submarine cables and pipelines), the new sea law has added two more freedoms to this list, viz., the freedom to construct artificial is lands and other installations and the freedom of marine sceintific research. However, states would be obliged to cooperate with other states in adopting measures to manage and conserve living resources. Thus in a way the traditional freedom of fishing is curtailed. The concept of the high seas too has undergone sea-change. Today only those parts of the sea that are not included in the territorial sea or internal waters of the states, in the EEZ or in the archipelagic waters of an archipelagic state may rightly be termed high seas. The high seas are to be reserved for peaceful purposes only.

Area. The *area* is the largest part of the Convention. This part establishes a legal regime for the exploration and exploitation of the bottom of the deep ocean in areas beyond national jurisdiction of any state. The area and its natural resources (polymetallic nodules composed of manganese, nickle, cobalt, copper, etc.) are the common heritage of mankind. Like the high seas it is open to use exclusively for peaceful purposes and for the benefit of mankind as a whole. However, all activities in the area would be under the control of an International Sea-bed Authority (ISA), with Jamaica as its Seat. All signatory states are its parties. The principal organs of the ISA are an Assembly, a Council and a Secretarial.

The Convention envisages the establishment of a paralell system for exploitation of resources on the sea-bed area. While the Authority (ISA) would conduct its own mining operations through its mining arm the Enterprise, it would also allow such rights to private and state ventures so that they could operate in tandem with the Authority.

Without doubt, the UNCLOS-III has achieved what may be described as a new Constitution of the Sea. The merits of the Convention are: one, it will help to maintain international peace and security by removing plethora of conflicting claims on the seas; two, it will facilitate navigation on the sea; three, it has translated the common heritage principle into fair and workable institutions and arrangements; four, it will promote international community's interests in the conservation and optimum utilization of the living resources; and five, it will promote social justice and contribute to the ushering in of the New International Economic Order by giving the land-locked and geographically disadvantaged states access of living resources of the EEZ of their neighbouring states.[11]

But the Convention has yet to come into force, for only 9 out of 60 (required) states have notified it so far.

SOVEREIGNTY OVER THE AIRSPACE

Just as high seas are unoccupied and open to all nations, the airspace above them and over unoccupied territory is free to all nations. But the airspace above a state territory including territorial waters falls under states jurisdiction. In other words, airspace over open sea and unoccupied territory is absolutely free. This rule is well recognised in international law. Until the First World War, however, there have been three theories on airspace over the occupied territory—both national or territorial. One theory treats airspace as a free zone. Another gives the lower zone of territorial airspace to the subjacent state. The third theory says that airspace to an unlimited height lies within the domain of the subjacent state. The last one says that airspace is within the sovereignty of the subjacent state subject to a servitude of innocent passage for foreign civil aircraft but not military aircraft. It found favour with most states during the First World War and has been generally accepted since them.

Before the First World War the subjacent state was regarded as sovereign on airspace over its territory. In the light of War experience a Convention for the regulation of Aerial Navigation was adopted at Paris in 1919. This Paris Convention is the foundation of Public Air Law and is also called the Constitution of the Air. It was a code for air navigation during peace times only. It established an International Commission for Navigation as permanent organisation under the League of Nations. This Convention recognised exclusive sovereignty of a state in the airspace above its territory including territorial waters, but in time of peace innocent passage was allowed to the private aircraft, if complied with the rules of the Convention. It could be prohibited for military and security reasons. The aircrafts were required to be registered and could be visited and their documents verified. Military aircraft could not fly over, or land on the territory without a special authorization. This Convention (1919) was followed by the Havana Convention of 1928, the Warsaw Convention of 1929 and the Convention of Rome (1933). The last one adopted uniform rules relating to damage caused by aircraft to the third party on the surface and to provide for compulsory insurance of aircraft.

Five Freedoms of the Air (The Chicago Convention of 1945)

In view of the requirements of the Second World War and also to cope with developing situation and to solve civil aviation problems an International Civil Aviation Conference was convened at Chicago in 1944. The Conference adopted five freedoms of the Air for Commercial air traffic rights. It was attended by about 50 states. These freedoms are:

1. Freedom to fly across foreign territory without lending on direct and reasonable route.
2. Freedom to land for non-traffic purposes.
3. Freedom to disembark in a foreign county traffic originating in the state of origin of the aircraft.
4. Freedom to pick up passengers, mails and cargo destined for the territory of that state whose nationality the aircraft possesses.
5. Freedom to carry traffic between two foreign countries.

Article 1 of the Chicago Convention recognized complete sovereignty of a state over the airspace above its territory subject to five freedoms. But the Convention was signed by 19 states only in the beginning, majority with England and India did not sign it. But by 1945, 33 states signed the first two freedoms. In 1951 this number rose to 41 states.

INTERNATIONAL CIVIL AVIATION ORGANIZATION

The ICAO was established in 1945. By 1959, 73 countries joined it. It replaced the International Commission For Air Navigation (1919). It decides disputes between members relating to the application of the Convention subject to appeal to the World Court.

LAW OF OUTER SPACE

Development in respect of outer space have added a new dimension to man's existence and opened new possibilities for the increase of his knowledge and the improvement of his life. In view of extraordinary scientific and technological progress since theSecond World War leading to launching of rockets, artificial earth-satellites into outer space and man's astounding feat of landing on the moon, the question of sovereignty into outers space came into focus of discussion.

As compared to the law of the sea, the law of outer space is still in its infancy. Nevertheless, the law of outer space has made the greatest progress of all branches of International Law during the last two decades. Today there are half a dozen treaties on the subject.

OUTER SPACE TREATY (1967)

The First Treaty on the principle of the activities of states on the exploration and use of Outer Space was adopted by the UN General Assembly in September 1967. Article I of this treaty lays down that the exploration of outer space including the moon and other celestial bodies shall be carried out for the benefit of all and shall be the "province of all mankind".

In 25 years after the launching of first artificial satellite by the Soviet Union (1957) four freedoms have emerged. These freedoms are:[12]

1. Equal right of all states to outer space and celestial bodies.
2. Right of sceintific research in any area of outer space.
3. Right to use any equipment and military personnel for sceintific research for peaceful purposes.
4. Right to use space techniques for practical purposes.

These rights are open to all. Article II of the Outer Space Treaty (1967) lays down that outer space (including moon and other celestial bodies) shall not be subject to national appropriation by claims of sovereignty. Article IV of this Treaty prohibits carrying in orbit around the earth nuclear weapons or any other kinds of weapons of mass destruction. Finally, states may not employ space techniques prejudicial to national sovereignty and other legitimate interests and rights of other states. Article VI of the treaty provides that the parties to the treaty shall bear international responsibility for national activities in outer space. In 1971, a Convention on International Liability for Damages caused by space objects was adopted by the General Assembly. Such damages include loss of life of other impairment of health or loss to property. The compensation would be determined in accordance with international law and principle of justice and equity. If no settlement of claim is arrived at through diplomatic nagociation a three members commission shall decide the amount of compensation. Article IX of the treaty requires that states conduct their research activities in a way so as to avoid harmful contamination and adverse changes in the environment.

An other Convention relates to agreement on the rescue of astronauts ('envoys of mankind') and return of objects launched in outer space (1968). There is one more Convention which demands registration of all objects lauched in outer space. In December 1979 the UN General Assembly adopted a Convention governing the activities of states on the moon and other celestial bodies. It is worth noting that it did not limit itself to use of such terms as "the Province of Mankind" and the benefit and interests of all countries, irrespective of the degree of economic and social development but went onto declare "the moon and its resources" to be the "common heritage of mankind".

The laws of the sea and outer space are components of the International Legal System; they complements each other in promoting cooperation and solidarity among states.

But the irony of the situation is that side by side with man's astounding exploration and exploitation of the peaceful potentialities of the oceans and outer space there are also disconcerting moves on the part of super powers to deploy devastating weapon system not only in the oceans but the outer space as well. Hence a fresh treaty banning the development and deployment of ocean-based (sea-launched nuclear cruise missiles) and space-based (anti-satellite weapons and "star war capability") weapon systems is urgently called for to preserve our planet.

REFERENCES

1. Svarlien, *An Introduction to the Law of Nations*, p. 155.
2. Jones, in M.P. Tandon, *Public International Law*, op. cit., p. 158.
3. I.C.J. Reports (1959), p. 4.
4. I.C.J. Reports (1969), p. 3.
5. Sorensen, M. (ed), *Manual of Public International Law*, New York, Macmillan, 1968, p. 472.
6. Higgins and Colombs, *Internationnl Law of the Sea*, 2nd ed., p. 108.
7. Rao, B.R. Papa, "Law of the Sea," *Indian Express*, dated 20 December, 1982,
8. Anand, R.P., "Winds of Change in the Law of the Sea" in R.P. Anand (ed). *Law of the Sea*, New Delhi, Radiant Pub., 1978, p. 39.
9. Kapoor, K.J.S.R., "Sea, Outer Space" in *World Focus*, Monthly, New Delhi January, 1983, p. 26.
10. Ibid., p. 26.
11. Ibid., p. 29.
12. Ibid., p. 29.

Chapter 9

Modes of Acquiring and Losing State Territory

Generally speaking, states have fixed territory. But at the same time new territory may be acquired and old one may be lost. The seven principal modes of acquiring territory are: (*i*) Occupation; (*ii*) Prescription; (*iii*) Accretion; (*iv*) Cession; and (*v*) Conquest—and the two Subsidiary modes are: (*vi*) Adjudication and Award; and (*vii*) Lease.

1. OCCUPATION

It is a means of acquiring territory not already in the dominion of any state. Oppenheim defines occupation as "an act of appropriation by a State of such territory as is not under the Sovereignty of another State."[1] According to Vattel, "all men have an equal right to things which have not yet come into the possession of any one and these things belong to the person who first takes possession." Such territory may be newly discovered or abandoned by the state formerly in control. Oppenheim calls possession and administration as the two essential facts that constitute an effective occupation. This is done by a settlement on the territory. This may also be done either by a proclamation of formal appropriation or by hoisting of a flag or by establishing some sort of administration. To Philmore and Lawrence, use of discovered area and settlement make occupation fully effective. In any case, the assertion of Sovereignty must be displayed. Besides, it must be actual and continuous.

Discovery

Mere discovery of land, however, is not enough, for it gives only an 'inchoate' title. To illustrate, Justice Max Huber, the arbitrator, in the Island of Palmas case[2] (1928) between the US and the Netherlands held that discovery alone could not suffice to prove Philippines' Sovereignty over the Island, because even if Spain originally had sovereignty over the territory, the Netherlands East Indies Company had administered it since eighteenth century thereby supplementing Spain. Since Spain had no title to the Island in 1898, the US could not acquire title from Spain as latter's successor over Philippines merely on the grounds of its discovery in the sixteenth century by Spain and its session to the US in 1898.

Proclamation

In the Clipperton Island Arbitration case[3] (1931) between Mexico and France, the King of Italy, the arbitrator, accepted the claim of France as legitimate in view of the French proclamation of sovereignty on November 17, 1858 against Mexico as France had enjoyed absolute and undisputable disposition of the territory. This judgment indicates that settlement or local administration is not an essential condition.

But in the Eastern Greenland case[4] (1933) between Denmark and Norway, the P.C.I.J. accepted the claim of Denmark over Greenland although Denmark could not exercise continuous and vigorous authority for certain handicaps. In 1931, Norway had proclaimed that it had occupied certain territories of Eastern Greenland which were terra nullius. The court while deciding the case observed: "a claim to sovereignty involves two elements: (1) the intention (animus) to act as a sovereign and (2) some actual exercise or display of authority. The court affirmed that occupation in order to create a title must be effective. This shows that mere discovery of an unappropriated territory is not sufficient basis to create a title to discovered territory unless it is brought under effective control. The court, therefore, held the Norwegian occupation as illegal in the absence of actual control.

The cases cited above lay down certain rules governing the title under occupation as a result of discovery. As regards the notification of occupation only Holland and Pitt Cobbet deem it necessary but Oppenheim does not thinks so.

Legal Status of Germany

As a result of Potsdam Agreement (1945), Germany came underf belligerent occupation of Four Powers, but it was not a case o subjugation. Its legal personality was only suspended and not extinguished. These powers never intended to subjugate the country. Starke is of the opinion that the "Allied Control System was of a provisional character. The act tantamounted to an act intermediate between belligerent occupation and subjugation."

Legal Status of Formosa (Taiwan)

Following her defeat during the Second World War, Japan made a renunciation of all rights, title and claim to Korea, Formosa and Pescadores. As soon as she signed the instrument of surrender,

Chiang Kai-shek, the ruler of China, took over the administration of Formosa. But in 1949 dispute arose between the Communist Government of China and Nationalist China headed by Chiang Kai-shek. With the result the Paking regime could not incorporate Taiwan in the mainland. That situation almost persists even today.

Man's Conquest of Moon and Mars

With the landing of US Spaceship Appollo II on the moon on July 20, 1969, a problem arose for international law as to whether the discovery or the conquest of moon constituted an acquisition through occupation. On this glorious occasion Nixon, the US President, had declared that "while it were the American astronauts who would become the first man in history to set foot on the lunar surface, the universe belonged to us all."[5] He added that there was no desire on the part of USA to claim sovereignty over the moon because of their discovery and landing. As a matter of fact, there cannot be any territorial claim on the moon arising from the landing of cosmic rockets or space shuttles or planting of flags, as both intention and establishment of some form of control—the necessary elements are absent. Mere discovery does not constitute acquisition through occupation, for it gives an "inchoate" title. Any way, there is not going to be any serious problem in the near future, for effective control and administration is still a far cry.

Arctic and Antarctic Regions

At the moment there is a great scramble for occupying the Polar areas. The Antarctic region covers one-tenth of the world surface. It is larger than Europe plus USA. It is the chilliest, dirtiest, windiest and least accessible. It was first sighted in 1820. It contains largest coal field and is abundant in oil, fish, gold and iron. It has 15 trillion cubic feet of gas. Its krill can triple world's fish catch. The recent entry of India into the polar circle has given a new twist to international scramble for the polar bonaza—a veritable Eldorado. At present the region is governed under the Antarctic treaty of 1959 which has been acceded by 14 countries. India is also one of the aspirants. She has already sent four expeditions to this region during the last three years. Like moon and mars the region cannot be brought under effective occupation. Hence for the present there is no problem for international law. As such the Antarctic treaty has already frozen all territorial claims in the region till 1991. It also provides for freedom movement and scientific exploration but the region is not to be used for military purposes. The widely held view is that the polar areas should be subject to international control. There is a proposal that they should be declared as common heritage of mankind by the UN General Assembly. However, notwithstanding this treaty there has been no renunciation of questionable claims in the area of the existing territorial rights.

2. PRESCRIPTION

Prescription is the acquisition of territory by an adverse holding continued for a certain length of time. International law, however, does not prescribe any definite period of time. It is an old saying that possession is nine points of the law. But possession must be peaceful, without protest and continuous for a long period. Grotius mentioned that "a possession beyond memory, not interrupted, nor disturbed by appealing to an arbitrator, absolutely transfers dominion." Vattel also recognised adverse possession if the owner had neglected his right or be silent. To take the case of Island of Palmas, it was Spain who had discovered it but due to her dereliction and negligence the Netherlands had been exercising undisputed sovereignty for over 200 years, hence the former's claim was not upheld. Prescription becomes complete if neighbouring nations come to an agreement by treaties.

Schwarzenberger sums up rules developed by the Permanent Court of Arbitration and Permanent Court of International Justice regarding prescription:[6] (1) State claiming title must display actual power; (2) Display of authority must be reasonably continuous; (3) Display of sovereignty must be peaceful; and (4) It should be made public, though there is no obligation of formal notification.

3. ACCRETION

A state can acquire territory through the operation of nature, when rivers silt up or when volcanic islands emerge in internal waters. New formation through accretion may be artificial—embankment, dykes or natural—drying up of a river or by the process of the sea. It also takes place by alluvion. It may also take the form of a delta (by the deposit of silt) or take the form of an island.

Incidentally, when an island is built within the maritime belt of a state, it has the effect of extending the maritime belt to an equal distance beyond the newly acquired territory. The addition in such cases is the property of the owner of the mainland. The Anna case (1805) is famous as an illustration of accretion. This Spanish vessel was captured by a British Privatcer near the mouth of Mississippe within three miles of the newly emerged mud island belonging to the US. The US contended that the capture was invalid as the ship was within the territorial water of the US when captured. Lord Stowell, who decided this case, accepted the American contention and concluded that the islands formed by alluvial action were the natural appendages of the coast on which they bordered and from which they were formed. He added that "the right of dominion does not depend upon the texture of soil."

4. CESSION

An act of cession means the transfer of title to definite portion of territory by one state to another by means of a bilateral transaction. Such transfer may be voluntary (sale, gift or exchange) or made under compulsion (as in war). The cession at times may be without compensation. For instance, when Venice was ceded by Austria to France in 1866 it was a voluntary transfer. But Alsace Lorraine was ceded to Germany by France under compulsion in 1871.

To take another example, Alaska was sold to America by Russia in 1867. The USA got Louisiana in 1800 and Florida in 1819 by sale treaty. England under Charles II got Bombay from Portugal as a result of marriage (dowry). The treaty of cession, however, must be followed by actual transfer of the territory to the new state. The latter can further cede it to a a third party after the ratification of treaty. But it cannot exercise its territorial supremacy thereon until it has taken physical possession.[7] Treaties, in case of cession, deal with matters like the status of inhabitants of the territory and adjustment of public debt, etc. They are at times followed by Plebiscite. For instance, the status of Saar was determined by this method in 1935. Similarily, Sylhet went to East Pakistan (Now Bangladesh) as a result of plebiscite in 1947.

5. CONQUEST AND SUBJUGATION

It is the acquisition of the territory of an enemy through military force in time of war. But as Oppenheim says: the conquest must be followed by annexation to get title. Such enemy state then ceases to exist. Annexation turns conquest into subjugation. To illustrate, Japan annexed Korea in 1910, Italy annexed Abyssinia in 1936 and so on. It is to be noted that military occupation alone does not bring about substitution of sovereignty as was the case of Germany in the

Second World War.

Until the Covenant of the League of Nations, war was a legal method to solve disputes and conquest a legal act of international law. But after the Paris Pact (1928) which renouncing war as an instrument of national policy, conquest lost its validity. For instance, the conquest of Manchuria by Japan in 1932 was treated as illegal. Similarly Israel's, annexation of Golan Heights (1981) was not recognised.

Both the Covenant and the Charter place an obligation to refrain from use of force against territorial integrity of another state. Thus title by conquest is illegal at the moment. But unfortunately international law does not provide any remedy for peaceful ejection of a colonial trespasser. That is why, India had to occupy Goa by force in 1961.

Starke adds one more way of acquiring territory.

6. ADJUDICATION AND AWARD

This occurs when a Conference of Victorious powers at the end of War assign territory to a particular state. To illustrate, the Kutch Award (1968) gave 300 sq miles to Pakistan and Radcliff Award determined the boundary of Bengal and of Punjab between India and Pakistan (1947).

7. LEASE

It is another mode of acquiring title to a territory. In case of lease the terms of treaty determine the amount nature of authority to be exercised by the lessee. But usually the sovereignty of the lessor state although resting legally with the lessor state is more nominal than real. Some of the well-known examples of leases are: the lease (99 years) of Hong Kong by China to Britain and of Kai Chow to Germany, the lease of Panama Canal zone to US by the Republic of Panama, the lease of a number of bases in the Caribbean Sea by UK to US (1941) and recently the lease of Teen Bigha to Bangladesh by India (1982).

COMPARATIVE STUDY OF DIFFERENT MODES OF ACQUIRING TERRITORY

While occupation, prescription and accretion are original modes. Cession and conquest are derivative modes of acquisition of territory.

To elaborate, in occupation sovereignty is operative with reference to the original owner of territory, while in conquest territory is under the ownership of another state.

Conquest and Cession

Conquest repressents a premature stage of claiming title to a territory. A legal title depends upon cession. When a military force occupies a state territory by conquest which is confirmed by a treaty of peace at the end of war, the legal title arises from cession and not conquest.

Loss of State Territory

The five common modes of acquiring a state territory also correspond to those losing it. Territorial sovereignty may be lost by (1) dereliction (abandonment); (2) prescription; (3) operation of nature; (4) cession and (5) conquest. Dereliction corresponds to occupation on the acquisitive side. But dereliction to be complete must comprise the actual abandonment of a territory and the intention of giving up sovereignty.

According to Oppenheim, besides cession, subjugation and prescription three other operations leading to loss of territory are volcanic eruption, revolt and dereliction. Revolt followed by seccssion is a mode of losing state territory. For example, Netherlands broke off from Spain under revolt in 1579, America broke off from Britain in 1776, Brazil revolted against Portugal in 1822 and Belgium against Netherlands in 1830, and more recently East Bengal broke off from Pakistan in March 1971. But the question at what time a loss of territory through revolt is perfected is not clear. Recognition of the territory acquired by a belligerent or insuregent is one of the ways which puts the stamp of the loss. Even then the mother country may not regard it as lost if only few countries recognise it.

REFERENCES

1. OPPENHEIM, *International Law*, op. cit., p. 555.
2. *American Journal of International Law*, 1928, Vol. 22, pp. 875-76.
3. *American Journal of International Law*, 1932, Vol. 26, p. 390.
4. P.C.I.J. Series A/B No. 53 (1933).
5. *Span*, New Delhi, American Embassy, July 1969, p. 25.
6. SCHWARZENBERGER, *A Manual of International Law*, Vol. I pp. 127-28.
7. OPPENHEIM, *International Law*, op. cit, p. 550.

Chapter 10

Intervention

Oppenheim defines intervention as "dictatorial interference by a State it the affairs of another for the purpose of maintaing or alterinig the actual condition of things."[1]

"It is the dictatorial or imperative interference by a state in the internal or external affairs of another state." In fact, intervention is more than mere interference. It must take an imperative form and should be forcible or backed by threat of force. In other words, the essence of intervention is force or threat of force as distinguished from good offices, advice or political influence. Its essence, therefore, is illegality and its justification is its success.

One of the oldest duties of a state is to obtain from interfering in the affairs of another state. Article 2 of the U.N. Charter implicitly prohibits intervention. Likewise, Articles 1 and 3 of the Draft Declaration on the Rights and Duties of States prescribe that all states shall refrain from intervention in the affairs of one another. International law enshrines the sovereign right of states within their respective domains. It is an inalienable right of every state to arrange its own affairs, adopt any constitution, and make any treaty. Thus, generally speaking, international law is opposed to intervention as such. Nevertheless, it does not prohibit intervention under all circumstances. The law permits it as a reaction against the violation of a state's rights by another state. Intervention, therefore, is not so much a right as the sanction of rights of states or as the policy through which states' rights are enforced.

KINDS OF INTERVENTION

According to Prof. Winfield, intervention is of four kinds.

1. Internal Intervention

It is interference in internal disputes between opposing sections of a country. To illustrate, Germany and Italy intervened in the Spanish Civil War of 1936-38 on behalf of General Franco. Some recent examples of this kind are the Soviet intervention in Afghanistan (1979-84), the US military intervention in Vietnam (1960-73) and in

Grenada (1983).

2. External Intervention

It is intervention by one state in the foreign affairs of another state. The entry of Italy in the Second World War siding with Germany against Britain provides an apt example of external intervention.

3. Punitive Intervention

It is a punitive measure falling short of War. It is in the nature of a reprisal for an injury suffered. A pacific blockade to compel the observance of treaty engagement is a sort of punitive intervention.

4. Diplomatic Intervention

When Russia, France and Germany jointly intervened to pressurise Japan to hand over Liaotung to China as per Shimonosheki Treaty of 1895, it was a good case of diplomatic intervention.

GROUNDS OF INTERVENTION

Of all things at once, the most unjustified and impolitic is an unsuccessful intervention. Let us here examine on what grounds intervention can be justified.

1. Self Preservation

One of the fundamental rights recognised by the Law of Nations is a state's right of self existence. To quote Hall, "in the last resort almost all the duties of a state are subordinated to the right of self-preservation." To be sure, self-defence is the supreme interest of a state. In order to toward off imminent danger to the security of state, a state can intervene and also justify it.

The well known cases of intervention on grounds of self-preservation are: (1) the Danish Fleet case (1807), (2) the Caroline case[2] (1837), (3) the Corfu Channel case[3] (1946), etc. In 1807, Britain seized a Danish fleet as Denmark was about to declare war on behalf of France after signing the Treaty of Tilsit (1807). The leading case of Caroline sets out the principle that governs the doctrine of self-preservation. In Canadian rebellion of 1837, Steamer Caroline used to send arms across Niagra river from America by the Canadian insurgents. The US Government did not prevent its operation. Consequently the British troops crossed the river and went within the American territory and destroyed Caroline. The US Government protested against it. In this connection the US Secretary of State, Webster, laid down the test on which intervention could be justified. He held that "necessity to be an excuse as a necessity of self-defence should be instant, over whelming and leaving no choice of means and no moment for deliberation." Since Britain could not prove this test, she had to express regret and apologise.

2. **Enforcement of Treaty Rights**

This is another ground which justifies intervention. It was on this ground that Britain intervened on behalf of Belgium when the latter's neutrality was violated in 1914 by Germany. The Soviet Union justified her intervention in Hungary (1956) and in Czechoslovakia (1968) on the basis of Warsaw Pact of 1955. However, few would agree with this justification. Even to this day, under the pretext of Warsaw Pact, as many as 30 divisions of the Red Army have been kept ready in Budapest, Warsaw and Prague. It is interesting to note that the late Brezhnev justified the Soviet intervention in Czechoslovakia in the name of what is called Brezhnev Doctrine under whose garb the Soviet Union would not allow real sovereignty in her satellite states. It would permit them only limited sovereignty. The thrust of this Doctrine is that the Soviet Union is determined to maintain Socialist Solidarity and to protect domestic socialist structure. The other super power too has intervened many a time in Latin American countries in the name of Bogota Pact (1948), e.g., her intervention in Guatemala (1954) to dislodge the regime of Arbenz.

3. **Grounds of Humanity**

Another justification for intervention is based on ground of humanity. It was on this ground that Great Britain, France and Russia jointly intervened in the War between revolutionary Greece and Turkey to put a stop to abominable atrocities by the Turks. Again, in 1960, Great Powers of Europe intervened in Lebanon to protect Christians from Islamic persecution there. However, as Lawrance has observed, "an intervention to put stop to barborous and abominable cruelty is a question of policy rather than of law."[4] The Charter by recognising the promotion of respect for human rights and fundamental freedoms as one of the principal objects marks a further step in the direction of elevating the principle of humanitarian intervention. The Charters permits intervention in the name of Championing human rights.

4. Balance of Power

Balance of power as a ground of intervention has been recognised by the Treaty of Westphalia (1648) Treaty of Utrecht (1713), the Congress of Vienna (1815) and Treaty of Paris (1856). The Crimean War of 1954-56 was undertaken jointly by Britain and France with a view to protect the Ottomon Empire, as Russia was trying to increase her influence in Turkey and thereby tilt the balance of power in her favour in South Europe. However, as far as international law is concerned this ground is not justified at least in theory, although it is a common practice even today.

5. Protection of Persons and Property Abroad

Sometimes a State has to intervene in a foreign country in order to provide protection to its nationals living in that country. To illustrate, Britain intervened in Egypt umpteen times till 1956 to protect its nationals and commercial interests. To give a recent example, the Reagan Administration justified the US invasion of Grenada (1983) by citing safety of about 1,000 Americans living there. Although the ostensible design was to destablise a regime deemed inconvenient and to install another one of a different dispensation. Is it not an Amercan version of the Brezhnev Doctrine? However, international law desires that normal channels must be tried before embarking on a course of intervention.

Other justifiable grounds of intervention are intervention against immoral acts, international nuisance, national insults, a collective intervention pursuant to the Charter and under international authority. The UN intervention in the Korean War (1950) is a case in point.

REFERENCES

1. OPPENHEIM, *International Law*, op. cit.. p. 305.
2. COBBET, PITT, *Leading Cases*, 5th Ed., p. 162.
3. I.C.J. Reports (1949), p. 4.
4. LAWRENCE T.J. in M.P. Tandon, *Public International Law*, op. cit., p. 144.

Chapter 11

Place of Individuals in International Law

The fact that individuals are normally the objects of international law does not mean that they are not, in certain cases, the direct subjects thereof. —*Oppenheim*

In the ultimate analysis, individuals alone are the subjects of international law. —*Kelsen*

The traditional international law was state-centric both in nature and content. It was based on the notion that the individuals were objects and not subjects of international law. International law was confined to rights and obligations of States *vis-a-vis* each other, the exception being the protection of aliens.

The term subjects of international law implies three things: (*i*) the incumbents of rights and duties, (*ii*) the entities having procedural privileges before International Tribunals, (*iii*) entities whose interests are regulated or affected by provisions of international law.

To resolve this controversy about the nature and scope of international law we should first know what the subject of law is, "Subjects of a law are those persons to whom rules of law are immediately addressed, that is to say, they are directly obligated by the rule of law." In other words, any person to whom law attributes rights and duties is the subject of law. "Objects are those persons to whom rights and duties are attributed by law, viz., objects are those things in respect of which these rights and duties are exercised." To distinguish between the two, Schleicher's analogy is very helpful. In this opinion, as per traffic law the driver is the subject and the speed of the automobile is the object of law.

States have always been recognised as subjects of international law. According to orthodox positivists, (the dominant view till recently) only States are subjects of international law and the individual persons are its objects. To them only States can make war or peace, can be partners in treaty or convention, can join international conference and organisation and can refer a dispute, to an international court. Did not the P.C.I.J. observe in Serbian Loans case that only States can prosecute any claim before it? The individual person has no legal standing except through his own State. He does not enjoy a locus-standi in international law. Thus according to this view "State alone are the wearers of international personality."[1]

Of course, primarily only States are the subjects of international law, but it is essential to recognise the limitation of the principle. Its correct meaning is that States alone can create international law, that international law is primarily concerned with rights and duties of States, and that States alone possess full procedural capacity before international tribunal. The principle does not go any further.

As opposed to the orthodox view there is another theory which goes to the maximum limit in the opposite direction. This theory, held by Kelson and others, maintains that in the ultimate analysis, individuals alone are the subjects of international law. To quote Westlake, "the duties and rights of the states are those of the men who compose them."[2] According to this theory, if international law regulates conduct of States, it actually regulates conduct of individuals. In the opinion of Stowell "fundamentally, the law of nations is a law of individuals enforced through the agency of the government of communities into which mankinds is apportioned." It cannot be denied that the individuals do enjoy benefits and burden under international law and that international law does create certain responsibilities and obligations for the individuals. There is even a tendency to confer rights on individuals even against their own States. The P.C.I.J. itself held in Danzig Railway Officials case[3] that Railway officials had a cause of action against Poland before it.

With the advent of the twentieth century the traditional (positivist) view became obsolete, and a powerful movement began for international recognisition of human rights and also the recognisition of the individuals as subjects of international law. The Pioneers of this movement are Lauterpacht[4] and Jessup, etc. Consequently the subject monopoly of the State disappeared in the post-War period and the individual person came to be regarded not only as an object but as the final end, a beneficiary and a potential subject of international law. Since the end of the First World War there is a tendency to create international machinery for the protection of fundamental rights. Treaties banning slavery, forced labour, protection of religious minorities and many rules of modern warfare show that individuals are now recognised as subjects.

Similarly after the Second World War also, the Paris Treaty of 1947 provided for equal treatment of minorities conferring rights directly upon individuals. Besides, there are a number of international conventions making rules for regulating the conduct of individuals.

As a result of modern developments in international law and the Charter of the United Nations the State-centric system of international law has yielded to the needs and aspirations of the people. According to Starke, "the individual has acquired a status and a stature transforming him from an object of international compassion into a subject of international right."

To substantiate, the Nuremberg principles as formulated by the International Law Commission fastened individual responsibility. Even Heads of State and responsible government officials are not absolved from responsibility. Now individuals can be punished for violation of international law, "for crimes are committed by men and not abstract entities, and only by punishing individuals who commit such crimes can the provisions of international law be enforced."

The United Nations is specifically pledged to promote universal respect for Human Rights and Fundamental Freedoms. The General Assembly adopted in 1948 a Draft known as The Universal Declaration of Human Rights and Fundamental Freedoms which was prepared by the Human Rights Commission. In 30 Articles it sums up the civil, political and religious liberties men have struggled for so long. The Declaration is deemed to be the common standard of achievement for all peoples and all nations. Subsequently, the General Assembly unanimously adopted two Covenants (1966) reaffirming political, civil, economic, social and cultural rights. By 1982 both the Covenants were ratified by no less than 80 countries. The second Covenant dealing with political and civil rights recognised the subject status of the individual by permitting him to petition to the 18-Member-Committee on Human Rights against his own State. But as of today only 34 States have accepted the Optional Clause of the Second Covenant.

The spill-over effect of the 1948 Declaration was strikingly manifested in the Convention for the Protection of Human Rights and Fundamental Freedoms drawn up at Rome in 1950 by the Council of Europe. The Rome Convention provided for a European Commission of Human Rights to which any of the parties may refer alleged breaches by another. An optional clause empowers the Commission to deal with petitions from individuals and groups. Completing the Structure is the European Court of Human Rights (at Strosbourg) whose jurisdiction, however, is limited to States that adopt the relevant option.[5] The Court is open to States and to the Commission, but not directly to the individuals, though the Commission may refer to it for final decision complaints lodged with it by individuals. It is significant to note that 14 out of 19 States have already recognised the competence of the Commission to deal with individual petitions and granted compulsory jurisdiction to the court.

Indeed, the European Court of Human Rights is a show window for regional protection of human rights. It exists not in name only; it is quite active and has already decided a number of disputes between the individuals and their respective States. The first case that it decided was in 1966 known as Lawless *vs.* Irish Republic. In another case between Neumeister and Austria, the court held that Neumeister had been detained for an excessive period before his trial and hence the Austrian State had violated Article 5 of the Rome Convention requiring trial within reasonable time. Again, in "Vagrancy Case" against Belgium the court found a breach of Rome Convention as Belgium provided no remedy for questining illegal detention. In an inter-state case between Republic of Ireland and UK, the court held the interrogation of prisoners in Northen Ireland as degrading.

Besides, European Human Rights Convention, there is also an American Convention on Human Rights (1969) which came into force in 1978, and African Charter on Human and People's Rights. The other international documents dealing with the protection and promotion of Human Rights are: International Convention on Prevention and Punishment of the Crime of Genocide (1948), Supplementary Convention on the Abolition of Slave Trade (1956), Convention on the Political Rights of Women (1952), Convention on the Elimination of All Forms of Racial Discrimination (1965), Convention on the Status of Stateless Persons (1954), Convention relating to Status of Refugees, Convention on the Elimination of all Forms of Distinction against Women (1981), Recently the International Bank of Reconstruction and Development has set up arbitral tribunal to hear disputes arising out of investment between States and nationals of other States. Besides, individuals enjoy right of petition under the Trusteeship system as well. However, individuals have no such right under extradition treaties even to this day.

But in spite of the Charter and other documents and Conventions in his favour Green observes that "the individual has still a long furrow to plough before he receives any recognition of his status under international law."[6] Sharing the same view Starke says: "the bulk of international law still consists of rules which bind states only and only in a minority of cases lawyers have to concern with individuals and non-state entities as subjects of international law." Admittedly, the individual still lacks procedural capacity under international law.

All told, the place of individual in international law is still very nominal but it would be wrong to maintained that international law is concerned with States solely. The modern practice has recognised individuals and non-state entities as having rights and becoming subjects to duties directly under international law.

REFERENCES

1. SMITH, SIR, FREDERIC in M.P. Tandon, *Public International Law*, op. cit., p. 258.
2. WESTLAKE, in M.P. Tandon, *Public International Law*, op. cit., p. 259.
3. P.C. I.J. Series, B, No. 15 (1928).
4. LAUTERPACH, H. (Ed.), *International Law and Human Rights*, 1950, pp. 69-70
5. ROBERTSON, A.H., *British Year Book of International Law*, 1950, p. 162.
6. GREEN, L.C. in M.P. Tandon, *Public International Law*, op. cit., p. 275.

Chapter 12

Nationality

Nationality is the character or quality arising from membership of some particular nation or State which determines the political status and allegiance of a person. According to Oppenheim, it is the quality of an individual of being a subject of a certain State, and therefore its citizen. Fenwick has defined nationality as "the bond which unites a person to a given State, which constitutes his membership in a particular State, which gives him a claim to the protection of that State and which subjects him to the obligations created by the laws of that State."[1] Nationality is the most important link between an individual and his state and it is because of this link that he enjoys the benefits of international law.[2] A man's nationality, however, is not necessarily the same from his birth to his death.

The question of the determination of nationality, however, comes within the domain of Municipal Law and not international law. Each state has a right to determine its national from whom it may claim allegiance. The right to nationality is not a natural right. On account of growing international intercourse and traffic conflict between different municipal laws is bound to occur. The Hague Condification Conference (1930) while adopting Convention on the Conflict of Nationality Laws left to each State to determine as to who are its nationals under its own law, which law is to be recognised by other States in so far as it is consistent with international conventions or customs and the principle of law generally recognised pertaining to nationality.

Incidents of Nationality under International Laws

According to Starke, the various incidents of nationality are: (*i*) the right to diplomate protection a broad; (*ii*) the responsibility of the state for its failure to prevent or punish wrongful acts by its national committed aboard; (*iii*) the duty to receive back on its territory its own nationals; (*iv*) duty of the national to perform military service for his state; (*v*) general right of a state to refuse extradition of its own nationals to another state requesting for their surrender; (*vi*) determination of enemy status in time of war according to the nationality of the person concerned, and (*vii*) exercise of jurisdiction by states on the basis of nationality.[8]

Mode of Acquiring Nationality

The first and foremost mode of acquiring nationality is by birth. It may be according to jus soli—the territory of birth or jus sanguinis—the nationality of the parents at birth or according to both. Germany and France adopt the test of parentage as the decisive factor for determining one's nationality. In Argentina, on the other hand, the decisive factor is the territory on which a child is born. Countries like Great Britain and USA adopted a mixed principle. But in 1982, a nationality law was passed by the British Parliament which negates the principle of jus soli hitherto adopted in UK.

The second mode of acquiring nationality is by naturalization. It is an artificial tie of allegiance between a person and the State where the person resides. There are six ways of naturalization and they are: (1) marriage-wife assuming her husband's nationality; (2) legitimization—the illegitimate child acquires nationality of the father; (3) option; (4) domicile—to illustrate, as per Indian law, a foreigner can acquire Indian citizenship by a stay of 5 years; (5) appointment—as Govt. official of another State and (6) application—by applying for nationality to the State authorities of another country.

The third mode of acquiring nationality is by resumption. Original nationality can be resumed on fulfilling certain conditions.

The fourth and fifth modes of acquiring nationality are by subjugation and by cession of territory. Through subjugation the annexed territory comes under the sovereignty of the conqueror and ipso facto its inhabitants would acquire the nationality of the conquering State. But now the position has undergone a change as a result of the Treaty for the Renunciation of War (1928) and the U N. Charter. Consequently, the nationals of an annexed territory are allowed option of nationality.

The Indian Citizenship Act (1955) provides for the modes of acquiring Indian Citizenship by birth, descent, registration, naturalization, and incorporation of territory.

LOSS OF NATIONALITY

According to Oppenheim, there are five modes of losing nationality, which are as follows:

1. **Release.** Some States like Germany, etc., grant their citizens the right to ask for release from nationality. Such release, if granted, denationalises the released individuals.

2. **Deprivation.** Certain States have framed some municipal laws the breach of which by its nationals results in the deprivation of their nationality. Under the American law, for instance, service in the army of a foreign State also results in deprivation of citizenship.

3. **Expiration.** In certain States on account of legislation, citizenship expires due to long stay aboard. For example, a naturalized American citizen loses his nationality by having a continuous residence for three years in a foreign State in which he was either born or was a national previously.

4. **Renunciation.** In the case of double nationality of children the municipal laws of certain States like Britain give them a right on coming of age to declare whether they wish to cease to be a citizen of one State. The British Nationality Act of 1948 permits renunciation in such a case except that such declaration is withheld during the War.

5. **Substitution.** According to the laws of certain States the nationality of their subjects is extinguished by their naturalization abroad. The British Nationality Act (1948), unlike the US Nationality Act (1962), however, does not automatically entail the loss of British nationality on the naturalization of a British subject in a foreign State.

The Constitution of India provides for the loss of citizenship in the following two circumstances:

1. A person who after the 1st March 1947 migrated from the territory of India to the territory of Pakistan shall not be deemed to be a citizen of India.

2. No person shall be a citizen of India if he has voluntarily acquired citizenship of any foreign State. The Indian Citizenship Act (1955) also provides for the termination and deprivation of citizenship by renunciation and naturalization.

DOUBLE NATIONALITY

Owing to the conflict of nationality laws it often arises that certain individuals possess double nationality. There is no uniform rule in different States as to whether nationality would be acquired by the nationality of the parents at birth (jus sanguinis) or the territory of birth (jus soli). Britain, USA and some Latin American States follow primarily the principle of jus soli. France, Germany and other European States adopt the principle of jus sanguinis. Owing to this conflict of nationality laws and their lack of uniformity it often happens that certain individuals come to posses double nationality. A frequent instance is the case of a woman who, marrying some one not of her own nationality, may retain her nationality according to the law of her own State and acquire the nationality of her husband according to the law of the State to which he belongs. In many State laws the wife's nationality follows that of her husband. But the US departed from this rule in 1922 in the case of Liza Alexander. Now the principle of the independent status of women has been supported by the Convention on Nationality of Married Women adopted by the General Assembly in 1957. Double nationality may also arise from birth in the territory of a State different from that to which the parents belong. To give illustrations, a child born of French parents in the United States is an American citizen jus soli, but the child is at the same time a French citizen jus sanguinis. His effective citizenship will then depend upon the jurisdiction within which he happens to be. In the United States, he is an American; in France a Franchman; in any other country he may be both. Similarly, a child born in Great Britain of German parents acqires two nationalities at the same time, i.e., British and German. This double nationality can, however, cease if the person on coming of age declares his allegiance. Likewise, when an American woman marries an Englishman, she acquires British nationality without losing American citizenship unless she makes a formal renunciation of her citizenship before a court dealing with naturalization of aliens. The legitimization of illegitimate children can also produce the same effect.

The Hague Codification Conference of 1930 provided that a person having double nationality might be regarded as its national by each of the States whose nationality he possesses and he could renounce one of them with the permission of the State whose nationality he wants to surrender. A third State shall recognise only the effective nationality of such persons.

Leading Cases

The leading cases on double nationality are the Canevaro case, Willian Mackanzie's claim, Kramer *vs.* Attorney General and Nottebohm.

In the Canevaro case[4] (1912) between Italy and Peru the facts were as follows: Rafael Canevaro was born on Peruvian territory and was accorded Peruvian nationality jus soli. But since he was born of an Italian parents as such he was also an Italian under the law of Italy jus sanguinis. In deciding this case of double nationality the Permanent Court of Arbitration observed: "as a matter of fact, Rafael Canevaro has on serveral occasions acted as a Peruvian citizen both by running as a candidate for the Peruvian Senate and particulariy by accepting the office of Consul General for the Netherlands after having secured the authorization of both the Government ȧs the Congress of Peru. Under these circumstances whatever Canevaro's status as a national may be in Italy, the Government of Peru has a right to consider him a Peruvian citizen and to deny his status as an Italian claiment." However, the claim of the Italian Government on behalf of his two brothers can upheld by the tribunal.

STATELESSNESS

The problem of statelessness has of late assumed importance due to conflict of laws relating to nationality. There have been cases where nationality has been lost due to failure of nationals of a certain State to return to their own country. For instance, many Russians lost their nationality after the Revolution of 1917, because they were not willing to return to Russia. A person may be destitute of nationality knowingly or unknowingly, intentionally or through no fault of his own. However, a stateless person is open to persecution and general hardship.

Oppenheim mentions several cases of statelessness. Even by birth a person may be stateless. To illustrate, an illegitimate child born in Germany of an English mother is actually destitute of nationality, because according to German law it does not acquire German nationality and according to British law, it does not acquire British nationality either. Again, all children born in Germany of parents who are destitute of nationality aqcuire the character of statelessness. Statelessness may also arise later by deprivation of nationality. All individuals who have lost their original nationality without acquiring another are, in fact, stateless.

The Hague Codification Convention of 1930 on the Conflict of Nationality Laws desired to end the State of statelessness but its provisions did not cut much ice, because of its non-ratification by a sufficient number of States. The Convention, however, provided that a child whose parents are unknown or who have no nationality or whose nationality is unknown are to have the nationality of the country of birth.

The State within whose territory such stateless persons inhabit can require them to leave the country. Since such persons belong to no country, they are deprived of the benefits that international law secures to the citizen of a State. Persons may also become stateless by the operation of newly framed nationality laws, as were many Indians after passing of citizenship laws by Ceylon and India after their independence. There were about 10 lakh such persons whose citizenship was to be determined. As per 1964 Agreement between Shastri and Srimavo Bandaranaike and subsequent Agreement of 1974 India was to take back 6 lakh persons in addition to natural increase and Sri Lanka to absorb 4 lakh within 15 years. The Pact of 1964 was extended by 2 years until October 31, 1981. As of December 31, 1984 Indian gave citizenship to 4 lakh plus 1 lakh plus 1/2 lakh and Sri Lanka gave citizenship to 2,30,000 plus 55,000 persons. The fate of 4 lakh persons is yet to be decided. A recent gesture of Jayewardene was its decision to make the remaining 93,000 Sri Lankan citizens.

The International Law Commission selected 'Nationality' including 'Statelesseness' as one of the topics for codification in 1949. It prepared Draft Convention on the elimination of future statelessness. The Draft Convention provides that a child who would otherwise be stateless shall acquire at birth the nationality of the country in whose territory it is born. Again, a person born board a vessel at sea shall have the nationality of the State whose flag the vessel flies. If such birth takes place on board an aircraft the nationality is to be that of the place where the aircaft is registered. It further provides that the loss of nationality resulting from marriage, legitimization or adoption shall be conditional upon acquisition of another nationality. No person shall be stateless on grounds of departure, staying abroad, or failure to register. Further, no person is to be deprived of his nationality on racial, ethnical, religious or political grounds, nor shall the transfer of territory automatically result in the loss of nationality by the inhabitants living on that territory.

In its sixth session (1954), the I.L.C. also observed that statelessness is inconsistent with the existing principle which postulates nationality as a condition of enjoyment by the individual of certain recognised rights under international law.

REFERENCES

1. FENWICK, *International Law*, op. cit., 1971, p. 301.
2. OPPENHEIM, *International Law*, op. cit., p. 640.
3. STARKE, *An Introduction to International Law*, op. cit., pp. 338-39.
4. FENWICK, *International Law*, op. cit., 1971, p. 305.

Chapter 13

Extradition

The term "extradition" denotes the process whereby one state surrenders to another state at its request a person accused or convicted of a criminal offence committed against the laws of the requesting state, such requesting state being competent to try the alleged offender.[1] According to Oppenheim, "extradition is the delivery of an accused or a convicted individual to the state on whose territory he is alleged to have committed a crime by the state on whose territory the alleged criminal happens for the time being."[2] This surrender of offender is made in compliance with a formal demand through diplomatic agents and in compliance with a treaty of extradition between the two states.

NECESSITY OF EXTRADITION

To the question whether a country of refuge should try the fugitive in its own courts or deliver him to the requesting state whose law has been broken, International law gives no certain answer. Some jurists—Grotius, Vattel and Kent among them—hold that a state is bound to give up such fugitives but the majority—Puffendorf and others—appear to deny such obligation. But mutual interests of states for the maintenance of law and order and the common desire to ensure that serious crimes do not go unpunished require that nations should cooperate with one another in surrendering fugitive criminals to the state in which the crime was committed. Further, there is an obvious advantage in prosecuting the offender in the country where the offence was committed because the relevant facts and evidence could be made available only in the requesting state. However, the universal practice of states is to surrender fugitive offenders only under extradition agreements and now few jurists affirm any general duty or perfect obligation. It is now generally agreed that surrender is a matter of comity and not of right. For example, Pakistan does not seem to be willing to surrender or punish two sets of Indian hijackers (1981 and 1984) of Indian aircrafts in the absence of extradition agreement between India and Pakistan, notwithstanding three Conventions on hijacking to which both are signatories.

There are two practical difficulties about extradition which have prevented the growth of a uniform rule on the subject. First, there is no agreement on the definition of certain crimes. Second, the possibility of the process of extradition being employed to get hold of a person who is really wanted not for an ordinary crime, but for a political offence. Modern states almost invariably excludde political offence from the operation of the law of extradition.

The Law and Practice of Extradition in Different States

The law of England appears to be strongly against surrender in the absence of treaty obligations. It does not warrant surrender without express statutory authority. Such authority is now provided by the Extradition Acts of 1870 (as amended in 1883, 1895, 1906, 1932 and 1935) but only in the case of specified offences and with regard to countries with which Extradition Treaty has been signed. The "United States" practice also shows that there is no legal right to demand surrender in the absence of a treaty. Further, the US is a party to the Montevideo Convention on extradition (1933) which stipulates extradition of a person charged with an offence constituting a crime in both the demanding as well as the surrendering states with a minimum penalty of imprisonment for one year. The Indian Extradition Act of 1903 (amended in 1962) lays down the procedure for the surrender of fugitive criminals after being satisfied that a *prima facie* case has been made out in support of the requisition. The Union Government can refuse to apprehend a fugitive criminal if the crime is of a political character. The Indian Act substantially follows the provisions of the English Extradition Act. In extradition cases there must be an extraditable person and an extraditable crime. Many states such as France, Germany, Italy, etc., have adopted the principle of never extraditing their own subjects who commit a crime abroad. But Britain and the US do not subscribe to this view. At any rate, no duty to return their own nationals is recognised unless the treaty expressly stipulates such surrender. The Geneva Convention of 1936 requires such State to prosecute its nationals for crimes relating to counter feiting of currency, drug trafficking, etc., even though the offence may have been committed abroad.

Necessary conditions for extradition or rules governing extradition.

1. **Exemption of political offenders.** If a fugitive criminal has done a political crime, he is not to be surrendered. The term "political offence", however, is not easy to define. In other words, the concept of political crime hangs precariously on the cliff of vagueness. But according to judicial decisions it has been established that to consti-

tute a political offence there must be two or more political parties, each seeking to impose a government of its choice or striving for political control, and the offence must be committed in pursuance of that objective. This exemption, however, excludes anarchists and terrorists (vide Meunier Case), as they reject law and political process in general.

Leading cases on political offence. In reCastioni (1890)[3], a Swiss subject had taken part in a political disturbance in Switzerland in the course of which he killed a Municipal Commissioner. In the extradition proceedings initiated on behalf of the Swiss Government, the British Magistrate committed Castioni to prison, because he did not accept his crime to be of a political nature. But on a writ of Habeas Corpus, the Divisional Court held that the act of murder was in furtherance of changing the government. The Queen's Bench Division, therefore, let off Castioni by holding that the offence was a political one, as it was "incidental to and formed part of political disturbance" and hence refused to order his extradition to Switzerland. But in another case—"Meunier" (1894)[4], the offender who had caused explosion in a Paris Cafe, his offence was not treated as a political one by Justice Cave of a British Court because the accused was an anarchist and hence his crime was beyond the scope of political offence. Again, in re Kolczenski and others an English Court held that the term "offence of a political character" was not exhaustive. The term must be considered in the context of circumstances under which the crime is committed. The facts of the case are as under:

In re Kolczenski[5] and others, seven members of the crew of a Polish fishing trawler, finding themselves under political supervision and suspecting punishment because of their political beliefs, placed the master and others of the crew under restraint and brought the trawler to an English port where they were detained on September 22, 1954 under the Aliens Order of 1953. The Warsaw Government sought their extradition. The British Magistrate found them guilty of revolt (treason) on the high seas, an offence listed in the schedule to the UK-Poland, Extradition Treaty of 1932. But when the applicants moved for writs of Habeas Corpus, the Queen's Bench Division held as follows:

It was held that the term "Political" must be considered according circumstances at the time. The present time was very different from 1890 when Castioni's case was decided. It was not then considered a treason for a citizen to leave his country and starta fresh life in another country. The charge of treason does not hold good in this case. The applicants in the present case adopted the only course open to them. The acts done by them were only with the object of leaving the country. They therefore committed an offence of a political character, for if they were surrendered they would be punished for a political crime. The court, therefore, decided that the applicants were exempted from surrender to the Polish State by virtue of Sec. 3 (1) of the Extradition Act, 1870 and writs of Habeas Corpus were issued. The significance of this case lies in the fact that it gives a wider meaning to the term "political offence" and enlarges the scope of exemption to political offenders. It maintains that offence in association with a political object or to avoid political persecution for political defaults are political crimes.

But the rule that political offenders are not extraditable is subject to an exception which is contained in the "attentate-clause" that says: "the murder of the Head of State of a foreign country or a member of his family is not to be considered a political crime." This rule was a sequel to Belgiam's refusal to extradite Jacquine who had caused explosion to murder Napoleon-III.

2. Military offence such as desertion, religious offencess and other trifling offences are also generally not subject to extradition proceedings.

3. The fugitive whose surrender is sought should not be tried for any offence committed prior to his surrender other than the offence mentioned in the request for extradition until he has been liberated and has had an opportunity of leaving the country. This is known as the principle of speciality. For instance, in the case of USA *vs.* Rauscher[6] (1886), Rauscher, a sailor, was surrendered by Great Britain to the US upon a charge of murder. But when he was tried on another charge and convicted, the Supreme Court on appeal quashed the conviction.

4. The crime must be an offence in both the requesting as well as the surrendering State. This is based on the Principle of double criminality. Extradition treaties generally embody a clause that acts punishable in both countries with specified penalities shall be extraditable.

To illustrate, in the Eisler Extradition case[7] (1949), Gerhart Eisler, an alien communist, convicted in America of some criminal offences fled from New York to England, while he was on bail. On a request from the US Government, the British police officers arrested him at Southampton. The British magistrate discharged Eisler from custody on the ground that the offence for which he has been convicted in America—(1) Contempt of congress and (2) making false affidavit to get permission to leave America—did not fall under the technical head of "perjury" in England. That is, the second offence was not a case of perjury in English law. This case emphasises the principle of double criminality.

5. A fugitive criminal who has been accused of some offence shall not be surrendered to the requesting state until after he has been tried and has served his sentence for the offence that he has committed in the state requested for surrender.

6. There must be reasonable *prima facie* evidence of the guilt of the accused. The requested state shall satisfy itself that the evidence submitted justifies *prima facie* judicial proceedings, e.g., in Sucha Singh's case (1965) this condition against the accused was satisfied by the Nepal Government before he was surrendered to India.

LEADINC CASE ON EXTRADITION

Eichmann's Case[8]

Adolf Eichmann, to a German War criminal, who carried out ruthlessly Hitler's anti-Semitic Policy escaped to Argentina after the defeat of Germany in 1945. Later on he was chased by the Israel's Police who abducted him in 1960. Since this way of getting his surrender (extradition by abduction) was against the established Practice, Israel had to apologise. Nonetheless, the Israeli Government did try Eichmann and sentenced him to death in 1961.

Trial of Eichmann

Eichmann was tried under the Nazi Collaboration (Punishment) law passed by the Knesset (Israeli Parliament). It was argued on his behalf that:

1. the Israeli Court had no jurisdiction to try crimes committed outside Israel and before its creation;

2. as the accused was captured in a foreign land and brought to Israel in violation of international law such illegal act had taken away her jurisdiction;

3. the accused had acted in the course of duty on behalf of a foreign State, that is, it was an act of State.

The Supreme Court dissmissed the appeal and found him guilty on the following grounds:

1. The accused was a fugitive from justice from the point of view of the law of nations. The crimes attributed to him were of international nature. By virtue of the principle of universal jurisdiction every country had a right to try him and such a jurisdiction was

vested in the State of Israel on its establishment as a Sovereign State in 1948. In trying him the court was functioning as an organ of international law. It was, therefore, immaterial if the crime in question was committed outside Israel and before the existence of Israel.

2. In the absence of the extradition agreement between Argentina and Israel, the accused could not claim immunity as a fugitive offender, particularly, as the accused was not a political criminal and Argentina had given him no right of refuge. The court observed that a fugitive had a right of immunity when he was extradited for a specific offence which was not an offence for which he was tried.
3. The contention regarding the 'act of State' was also rejected in view of the principles laid down in Nuremberg Military Tribunal that individuals were also responsible for war cirmes.
4. The Supreme Court also observed that the right of asylum and immunity belonged to the country of asylum and not to the fugitive offender.

It is an important case of national punishment for an international crime.

Tarasov's Case[9]

V.S. Tarasov was a sailor on a Russian Oil Tanker. He was charged for theft of Rs 700 on Novemher 25, 1962. He jumped on an American Steel Surveyor on 25th November. An inquiry was made by a Judicial Magistrate (N.L. Kakkar) as per Section 5 of the Indian Extradition Act, 1962. In his judgement on March 29, 1963, no *prima facie* could be established against Tarasov on the basis of the report submitted by M.A. Brown, the Captain of the ship (Tanker). Since this evidence against him was not convincing, his extradition was not allowed to the Soviet Union by the Indian Government, and Tarasov was acquitted on March 29, 1963. The Magistrate did not accept the argument of the Soviet authority that there existed an extradition agreement between the two states since the extradition Act was extended to Soviet Union by notification.

Savarkar's Case[10] (1910)

Vinayak Damodar Savarkar was being transported in 'Morea' (P & O Steamer) to India for trial on a charge of night reason and abetment of murder. He managed to step out at Marseilles through the port hole of a water closet. But he was captured by a French Police man who handed him over to the Captain of Morea without extradition proceedings. Being a political offender France demanded him back but the British Government refused to surrender. Ultimately, the matter was referred to the Permanent Court of Arbitration which decided the case in favour of Britain, holding that she had no duty to restore Savarkar, though there was some irregularity. The decision received trenchant criticism. But "according to circumstances, the decision was not wrong", as Lawrence has commented.

ASYLUM

The conception of asylum in international law involves two elements: (*a*) shelter and (*b*) a degree of active protection on the part of authorities in control of the territory of asylum.[11] Asylum is the right of a Sovereign State to grant shelter and protection to a foreigner and to refuse his extradition. Asylum may be territorial as well as extra-territorial. The former is universally accepted but there is no agreement on the latter in international community.

Territorial Asylum

Territorial Asylum is not usually granted to ordinary criminals. It is given only to those who apprehend prosecution, or who are wanted for political crime. Some of the well known cases of such asylum are Emperor Wilhelm-II of Germany in Holland, Dalai Lama of Tibet in India, etc. Under Article 14 of the Universal Declaration of Human Rights every person has a right to seek and enjoy in other countries asylum from persecution.

Subsequently, the General Assembly said in the Declaration on Territorial Asylum (1967) that the grant of asylum is a humanitarian act and, as such, it cannot be regarded as unfriendly by any other state. But it added (Art. 4) "States granting asylum shall not permit persons who have received asylum to engage in activities contrary to the purposes and principles of the UN." Respect for the "territorial integrity and political independence of any state" ranks among them. Finally, in 1970 the General Assembly adopted a Declaration of Principles of International Law Concerning Friendly Relations and Cooperation among States. One of them says that "No state shall assist or tolerate subversive, terrorist or armed activities directed towards the violent over throw of the regime of another state or interfere in civil strife in another state." In the light of these rules India has good reason to be resentful of the laxity and indulgence which Britain, the US, Canada and Pakistan have shown in their territories towards advocacy of violence, open incitement to assassination and secession in India by

Sikh leaders like Dr Jagjit Singh Chauhan, Dr G.S. Dhillon, etc. Likewise Tamil refugees have no right to advocate use force against Sri Lanka on Indian soil and still less to plan or mount armed attacks from here.[12]

Extraterritorial Asylum (Diplomatic Asylum)

The asylum given by a foreign diplomatic mission or a warship is called extraterritorial asylum. International institutions like the UN and Specilized Agency Headquarters do not have such a right. According to Havana Convention (1928) asylum should be denied to persons accused of common crimes and for deserters from army and navy, and to be given only to political offenders.

Leading Cases. Senor Haya de la Torre,[13] a Peruvian political leader was given asylum in the Colombian Embassy in Peru in 1949. The Embassy requested for the safe conduct of Torre to leave the country. But the Paruvian Government rejected the request and hence the International Court of Justice was referred which held the asylum to be irregular, and hence Peru was not obliged to accept the request.

A decision to grant diplomatic asylum involves a derogation from the territorial Sovereignty of State. Although the Indian Mission at Kathmandu itself had given asylum to King Tribhuwan of Nepal (1950). She had to reconsider the issue when Aziz Zade, a Russian citizen, sought refuse in the US Embassy at New Delhi, and then placed under the Protection of the Indian Government. Later he was allowed to go to UK, as desired. India refused to recognise the right of diplomatic asylum. It urged all the missions established in India not to afford asylum, as India did not recognise such right. It is of the opinion that giving diplomatic asylum is not within the purposes of diplomatic assignment. The World Court too frowns on diplomatic asylum but at the same time it has ruled that there is no obligation on a nation to surrender the fugitive either.

Asylum on foreign worships. It is granted only to political refugees. The Havana Convention forbids it on warships and military aircrafts.

REFERENCES

1. STARKE, *An Introduction to Internatianal Law*, op. cit., p. 348.
2. OPPENHEIM, in Chavan, R.S., *An Approach to International Law*, New Delhi, Sterling Pub, 1978, p. 144.
3. FENWICK, *International Law*, op. cit., 1971, p. 394, (1891), 1 Q.B., p. 149,
4. (1894) 2 Q.B., p. 415.
5. (1955) 1 Q.B. p. 540.
6. FENWICK, *International Law*, op. cit., 1971, p. 391.

7. TANDON, M.P. *Cases in International Law*, Allahabad, Allahabad Law Agency, 1954, p. 183.
8. GREEN, L.C,, *International Law through Cases*, London, Stevene 1970, p. 239.
9. MAHAJAN, V.D., *Public International Law*, Delhi, Eastern Book Co., 1973 p. 766.
10. FENWICK, *International Law*, op. cit, 1971, p. 388.
11. STARKE, *An Introduction to International Law*, op. cit, p. 354.
12. NOORANI A.G. 'Law and Foreign Dissent,' *Indian Express*, dated January 12, 1985.
13. [ICJ Reports (1951), p. 71]

Chapter 14

Treaties

The modern international society rests upon agreements and conventions. The strands of interstate relations are woven into an intricate web of treaties, agreements and conventions. No wonder, treaties have become the most important source of law. A treaty is an agreement between international persons creating contractual rights and obligations. It is a formal communication through which a State acknowledge a commitment to another. Following Starke's definition, Article 2 of the Vienna Convention on the law of Treaty (1969) defines it "as an agreement whereby two or more states establish or seek to establish relationship between themselves governed by International Law."[1] Treaties are known by several names, such as Convention, Protocal, Statute, Declaration, Final Act, General Act, etc.

Kinds of Treaties

According to objects treaties may be political, commercial, social. Other varieties of treaties are, treaties of guarantee, neutrality, cession or extradition. M.C. Nair has classified treaties[2] as follows:

1. Treaties having the character of conveyance.
2. Treaties having the character of contracts—special matters.
3. Law making treaties: (*a*) Treaties creating constitutional law like statute of World Court, Leaugue Covenant, U.N. Charter. (*b*) Pure lawmaking treaties such as labour convention, etc. and (*c*) Treaties akin to charters of incorporations. The lawmaking treaties, however, involve two operations:

(*i*) legislative operation whereby rules are laid down and

(*ii*) undertaking of contracting parties to conform to those rules.

Some of the examples of lawmaking treaties are Treaty of Westphalia (1648), Final Act of Vienna Congress (1815), Declaration of Paris (1856), Suez Canal Convention (1888), Barcelona Convention (1921), Pact of Paris (1928), Montreux Convention (1936), League Covenant (1919) and the UN Charter (1945), Vienna Convention on the law of Treaties (1969), Third Sea Law Convention (1982), etc. Such treaties are called 'international legislation'. It is worth mentoining here that only international persons (including the United Nations) can enter into treaties.

Contracts and Treaties

Contracts are agreements between individuals which can be imposed by courts of law. The sanction of a contract is state and its authority. Again, in a contract there is free offer, free acceptance and a valuable consideration amongst the concerned parties but this may not be so in case of a treaty. The validity of a contract is quetionable if violance, threat or duress is exercised. But in a treaty duress had been recognised in the conclusion of treaties, for a long time. The Victor could dictate terms to the vanquished. In a treaty consideration may be inadequate and unequal. For instance, Treaty of Versailles was regarded as treaty alright, although it was dictated and signed on the point of a bayonet. But now a treaty cannot be concluded as a result of violence of intimidation. It is not binding if based upon material error or misrepresentation of facts. Article 103 of the Charter says that obligations under the Charter shall prevail over any other obligation. Thus immoral treaties are not binding. Similarly, Article 53 of the 1977 Vienna Agreement in respect to concluded treaties states that a treaty shall be considered null and void if it conflicts with a definte rule of international law.

Conclusion of Treaties

Even though sometimes oral agreements can be sufficient for the conclusion of a treaty, formal requirements however, are:

1. A party to a treaty must have a treaty making capacity; it must be an international person.
2. Accrediting of representative who is sent with Full Power Instruments.
3. Negotiation may be bilateral or multilateral.
4. *Signature*—unless subject to ratification, a treaty comes into force after signature.
5. *Ratification*—not all countries provide for it. But where it is provided treaties become obligatory only after ratification. Ratification, however, is not a legal but a moral duty. For instance, the US failed to ratify the Versailles and the SALT-II Treaties. Ratification, however, has a retrospective effect, so as to make the treaty binding from the date of its signature.
6. *Reservation*—reservation to be applicable must be acceptable to other parties. Further, it should be compatible with Convention.
7. *Accession of adhesion*—a third party can be adherent later on.
8. *Commencement of treaty* - in multilateral Conventions a prescribed number of adherents are required.
9. *Registration*—treaties must be registered at the Headquaters of

the UN. The UN authority can be invoked in case of treaty voilation only if it is registered with the UN as per Article 102 of the Charter.

10. *Revision and amendment of treaty*—treaties can be revised and amended by the agreement of parties concerned.

Termination of Treaties

Treaties can be terminated on the following grounds:

1. On the expiry of the specified period.
2. When the object of a treaty is fulfilled.
3. By mutuacl consent.
4. Due to non-performance of certain essential conditions by either of the parties as provided in the treaty Article 60 (1) of the Vienna Convention on the law of Treaties says: "a material breach of a bilateral treaty by one of the parties entitles the others to invoke the breach as a ground for terminating the treaty or suspending its operation.
5. When the obligation becomes in comparible with the UN Charter.
6. When war breaks out—nevertheless, provisions compatible with a state of hostilities will continue.
7. When one of the party is extinguished by annexation or merger with another country.
8. Force Majeure and impossibility of performance.
9. When the doctrine of rebus sic stantibus is applicable.
10. Withdrawl of parties and thereby reducing the number of signatories to less than prescribed.
11. By denunciation—if provided in the treaty.

Here it is relevant to mention that internal legislation is no ground for termination of an agreement. Article 27 of the Vienna Convention on the Law of Treaties clearly states that a party may not invoke the provisions of its internal law as justification for its failure to perform a treaty. To take a concrete example, the US Nuclear Non-prolification Act (1978) provides that "after a grace period ending March 10, 1980, a recipient of US nuclear exports must have all its nuclear activities under international safeguard as a condition of continued export." Thus by invoking an internal legislation the US has backed out from its commitment to supply enriched uranium to India till 1993 as provided in the Tarapur Agreement of 1963.

Rules Governing Treaty Observered

Pact a Sunt Servanda and Rebus Sic Stantibus. These are two

doctrines governing treaties which apparently challenge each other. Let us examine, how both the doctrines are accommodated in international law for the application of these conflicting doctrines may create a difficult situation at times.

The doctrine of Pacta Sunt Servanda is borrowed from the Roman law. It implies sanctify of contract. It implies, that parties are bound to observe a contract in good faith. In other words, states are bound to carry out in good faith the obligations they have assumed by a treaty. The sanctity of treaties is one of the oldest and doubtless the most fundamental rules of international law. Commenting on this doctrine Fenwick writes: "unless pledged words of a state could be relised upon, the relations of entire international community would be imperilled and law itself would disappear."[3] Speaking in the same vein, Prof. Lauterpacht comments: "the rule that compact must be kept is certainly one of the bases of the legal relations between members of any community.[4] Article 2 of the Charter also states: "all members shall fulfil in good faith the obligations assumed by them in accordance with the Charter. The rule of good faith is reaffirmed in Article 26 of the Vienna Convention of 1969. But at the same time the notion that in certain cases the law will refuse to continue to give effect to originally valid contract is common to all systems of jurisprudence.

Doctrine of Rebus Sic Stantibus. This doctrine too is borrowed from the Roman law. In Roman law every contract was subject to an implied condition. The result of this implied condition was that a contract remained binding only if circumstances remained the same. In international law the doctrine connotes that when the existence or development of a state conflicts with its treaty obligation, the latter gives way. It allows termination of a treaty on the ground of a fundamental change of circumstances. Every treaty does imply a condition, that the parties should have right to demand release from obligations. After all, state cannot allow themselves to be sacrificed at the alter of Pacta Sunt Servanda.

Although a numbers of writers such as Hall and Lawrence, Treitschke, Heffler support the doctrine but at the same time they admit that its scope and application are uncertain. Juristic opinion is far from uniform as to the nature of the doctrine. Consequently the doctrine has become "an enigma of international law,"[5] to quote Starke. The old writers such as Grotius, Vattel and Bynkershoek held that a change of circumstances did not affect the promise unless it was patently clear that the original circumstances were a part of the consideration of the contract. In the opinion of Oppenheim, the Clause does not give a state this right immediately upon the happening of a vital change of circumstances to declare itself free from obligation but only when other concerned parties agree to it. Of course if they refuse to reconsider it, it is justified. However, it is to be noted that the doctrine has not been recognised by international Courts and Tribunals As regards the League of Nations, Article 19 of the Covenant provided that if a treaty become in applicable and threatened peace it could be revised with the unanimous approval of all the contracting parties. It means the League allowed the application of doctrine but not unilaterally. The League, therefore, protested when Germany repudiated the Versailles Treaty in 1936. The U.N. Charter, however, does not have such specific provision. Yet Article 14 allows revision of treaty if peace is threatened or if it impairs the general welfare or friendly relations, and as such the General Assembly canr ecommend such revision. The matter is now finally dealt with in Article 62 of the Vienna Convention of 1969 under the heading "fundamental change of circumstances", which involves both subjective as well as objective test for the discharge of treaties in this ground.[6]

There are several instances in which the doctrine of Rebus Sic Stantibus was invoked. In 1870, Russia denounced the Block Sea Clauses of the Treaty of Paris (1856). But when Great Britain protested against it a Conference was called at London. Though the Conference released Russia from neutralization of Black Sea and restrictions on keeping armed vessels but only with the consent of the contracting parties. In 1871, Britain, France, Italy, Russia, Prussia, Austria and Turkey subscribed to the rule that "no power can liberate from the engagement of treaty, nor modify the stipulation, thereof unless it secures the consent of the contracting parties by means of an amicable understanding." Turkey applied it in 1936 and got the Lausanne Treaty (1923) on the status of Bosphorus and Dardanelles replaced by the Montreux Convention of 1936. Similarly, in 1950, Egypt contended that the Anglo-Egyptian Treaty of 1936 had out lived its purpose and got it replaced by another 7 years Agreement in 1954. Incidentally, this agreement was abrogated by President Nassier of Egypt in 1956 in view of thd Anglo-French aggression in 1956. In a more recent dispute between Iraq and Iran over the Shatt-al-Arab boundary line, Iran denounced the Iraqi-Iranian Treaty of 1937 and demanded a fresh agreement. But Iraq did not oblige. Subsequently, the issue was resolved by a fresh Treaty between the 2 countries (1975) which was based on the 1913 Constantinople Accord. This time (1980) Iraq denounced the agreement of 1975 followed by an attack on Iran in September 1980 and the war between the two countries is still going on.

These illustrations go to show that the doctrine has a very limited application. It simply gives the parties the right to demand a revision or termination or an agreement. The operation of this principle is necessarily limited for the simple reason that it is the function of law to enforce contracts or treaties even if they become burden some to the parties bound by them. To quote Brierly "every system of law has to steer a course between the dangers of impairing the obligation of good faith by interfering with contractual engagements and of forcing oppressive or obsolete contracts.[7] He further observes that there seems to be no recorded case in which the Clause has been accepted by both the parties. All told, a peaceful wayout of such predicaments awaits the development of an authoritative international couEt with compulsory jurisdiction.

REFERENCES

1. STARKE, *An Introduction to International Law*, op. cit., p. 399.
2. MCNAIR, *British Year Book of International Law*, 1930.
3. FENWICK, in M.P. Tandon, *Public International Law*, op. cit., 1971, p. 312.
4. LAUTERPACHT, H. in M.P. Tandon, *Public International Law*, op. cit., p. 313.
5. STARKE, *An Introduction to International Law*, op. cit., 4th Ed., 1958, p. 313.
6. STARKE, *An Introduction to International Law*, London, Butterworths, 7th Ed., 1972, p. 442.
7. BRIERLY, *The Law of Nation*, London, Q.U.P., 6th Ed., 1963, p. 339.

Chapter 15

Agents of International Intercourse

International relations are normally conducted through diplomatic agents, consuls, and other agents appointed by states. Today almost all states are represented in the foreign countries by such agents. Since now direct negotiation can take place between foreign ministers and heads of states, thanks to the present era of instant communication, diplomats are certainly losing stature, but their importance cannot be under estimated.

Diplomatic Agents are the official envoys sent on the mission of conducting relations with the foreign states to which they are accredited. The rules relating to diplomatic intercourse between nations has formed a part of international law since ancient times. The records of ancient China, India, Egypt show that ambessedors were frequently, if not regularly, were sent and received by these countries. They enjoyed great respect and their offices were regarded of a sacred nature.

The origin of organised diplomacy is traced to the relations among the city states of ancient Greece. The Greek city states almost approached our own system of regular diplomatic intercourse. But the Romans, however, did little to develop the art of diplomacy although they made important contributions to international law. Diplomacy as an organised profession arose in Itlay in the late Middle Ages, and by the middle of the 17th century sending of permanent representatives had become the rule. Diplomates from all countries graced the court of Louis XIV (1643-1775), for about three hundred years of diplomacy could be characterised as the diplomacy of the court. But by the late 18th century, the three revolutions—Industrial, American, and French—had ushered in a new era of diplomacy. The voice of people for the first time began to be heard; and thus growing democratic control made the duties of diplomats rather complicated.

FUNCTIONS OF A DIPLOMAT

Diplomacy functions through a labyrinth of foreign office, embassies, legations, consulates and special missions. It is said that a diplomat is the eyes and ears of his government. He is an agent of mutual adjustment between the ideas and forces upon which nations act. According to Palmer and Perkins, a diplomat performs four basic functions[1]: (1) Representation; (2) Negotiation; (3) Reporting; and (4) Protection of the interests of the nation and its citizens in foreign lands.

Representation

A diplomat is the normal agent of communication between his own foreign office and that of the state to which he is accredited. This representation is of three kinds—symbolic, legal and political. He performs the symbolic function of the diplomatic ceremonial. He is the legal agent of the government he represents. His acts possess legal value. He may cast his vote at international conferences in the name of his government.

Negotiation

Diplomats are by definition negotiatiors. Negotiation is the pursuit of agreement by compromise and direct personal contact. Their duty is to drait a wide variety of bilateral and multilateral agreements, treaties, conventions, protocols another documents of a political, social and economic nature.

However, because of ease and developments in communications and the increasing resort to multilateral diplomacy diplomats are losing their former importance and latitude. They have little freedom as negotiators. Today major international agreements are made directly by foreign ministers. Again diplomats are more closely bound to foreign offices by detailed instructions and constant communications by cable and trans-oceanic phones. But still it is too early to say that they are simply "glorified messenger boys" or "telephone girls" at the end of a wire. The value of the personal factor in diplomacy is even now very great. All the same, his role as a negotiator has considerably diminished.

Reporting

Diplomats are required to keep to their government posted with developments in the accredited states. Their reports are the raw material of foreign policy. They cover subjects from technical studies to the appraisal of the changing psychology and moods of the nation to which they are sent. For example, legislative programmes, public opinion, market conditions, production trends, tariffs and other laws are some of the matters on which they report. Therefore, a diplomat must be a man of keen observation, sound judgement and accurate description. It is upon the reliabillty of his report and soundness of judgement that the success or failure of foreign policy of his government depends.

Protection of National Interest and Nationals Abroad

The next duty of a diplomat is to look after national interests as interpreted by policy makers and according to treaties and principles of international law. They have to protect the interests of business men and other nationals who are living or travelling abroad and to prevent any sort of discrimination against them in foreign lands. Thus the functions of diplomacy in the modern age are many and complex, perhaps more so than even in the past.

CLASSIFICATION OF DIPLOMATIC AGENTS

During the 17th and 18th centries there were conflicts between the large and small states regarding precedence in the ranks of their ambassadors. The personal vanity of monarchs and the diplomatic agents and the political ambition of states brought about constant struggle for the enhancement of national prestige by trying to secure relatively better positions in the warrant of precedence.

In 1815, efforts were made at the Congress of Vienna to avoid conflicts amongst diplomats arising out of their ranking and to prevent other inconveniences by framing rules regarding classification of diplomatic personnel, protocol, forms of correspondence, and also immunities and privileges of diplomates.[2] According to the rules of the Congress of Vienna diplomatic hierarchy consisted of four classes: (1) Ambassadors, papal Legates and papal Nuncios and High Commissioners; they all enjoy direct audience with the head of State to which they are accredited, and they are called His or Her Excellancy as of right; (2) Envoys Extraordinary and Ministers Plenipotentiary; they are called "excellancy" by courtesy only as they are not personal representatives of the heads of state they come from; (3) Ministers resident (added by the Congress of Aix-la-Chappelle in 1818); (4) Chargé-d' Affaires. Now the second and third grades are merged in a single class know as "Envoys Extraordinary and Ministers Plenipotentiary by the Vienna Congress of 1961. Hence the Ministers Resident are deleted from the classification of diplomats.

It is worth mentioning here that no state is under obligation to send a particular grade of representative, but customarily small states do not appoint representatives of first class.

Ambassadors and Ministers, however, constitute a fraction of the total number of diplomats, most of whom are career officials or non-career specialists. Lesser diplomats cannot be classified. Only three ranks are recognised and these are: (1) Counsellors of embassy or legation who rank highest among the staff; (2) Secretaries of an Embassy ranked as first, second and third secretaries; and (3) Attaches who may be junior career officers or non-career persons serving on a temporary basis.

Diplomatic Rules and Procedures

Diplomacy is still conducted on the basis of a code that has evolved over many centuries. Some of its rules are made into writing, such as those laid down in the famous Reglement of 1815 or the Havana Convention of 1928, and the Vienna Convention of 1961.

Appointment and Reception of Diplomats

Regarding appointment, each state may adopt its own way. Yet certain generally recognised procedures are observed. As a rule, the nomination of a diplomat is made public only after the approval known as agrèment is secured from the country to which he is being sent. Sometimes approval may be refused. Before a diplomat leaves to take up his assignment he is furnished with certain important papers, diplomatic passports and a letter of credence. The letter of credence, which is a diplomat's formal commission, is signed by the head of the state and is addressed to the head of the state to which he is accredited. In the case of Chargè-d Affaires, the letter of credence is addressed by the foreign secretary or minister to his counterpart.

Ceremony of Presentation

A diplomat gets audience of the Head of State through its foreign minister. At that time a brief speech is made first by the envoy and then by the head who accepts the letter of credence. Then he confers with the foreign minister and other important leaders of the government and visits his colleagues of the diplomatic corps.

Termination of Diplomatic Mission

There are various ways of terminating a diplomatic mission. Besides resignation, or death, the other ways are recall or dismissal. A government may itself recall or it may be asked to do so. The receiving state may declare an envoy as persona non grata, and request his home state for his recall. If he is even then not recalled, such an envoy may be dismissed. However, dismissal is resorted to only in rare cases. A state can request for a recall of a diplomat if he is found to interfere in the internal affairs of the country of his accreditation or is charged with spying, espionage, subversive or such other undesirable activities.

Diplomatic relations and diplomatic mission come to an end during war between the countries concerned. For instance, during the Indo-Pak war (1971), the diplomatic relations were broken and the diplomatic missions were withdrawn. Similarly, during the Sino-Indian war of 1962, their ambassadors were withdrawn by both the countries.

PRIVILEGES AND IMMUNITIES

By long custom and practice diplomatic agents have been regarded to possess a sacred character in consequence of which they have been accorded special privileges and immunities. The reasons for this special status are two-fold: (1) Diplomats are personal representatives of their Heads of states, of their governments and also of the people of their countries; (2) In order to carry out their duties satisfactorily they must be free of certain restrictions imposed by local laws. These privileges and immunities were sanctioned by long custom and adopted in the Havana Convention of 1928. The Vienna Convention of 1961 has codified these well established rules of immunities and privileges. Articles 20 to 36 of the Convention deal with the immunities and privileges enjoyed by a diplomatic agent and the premises of his mission. They are as follows:

Personal Immunities

The person of a diplomat is inviolable, and in case of an affront against him, international law requires the foreign state to offer prompt apology and redress (Article 29). It also requires the wrong-doer to be punished. But such a protection is not available to a diplomat who unnecessarily commits an assault first or exposes himself to danger.

Exemption from Criminal Jurisdiction

Diplomates are completely immune from the criminal jurisdiction of a foreign state. They cannot be presecuted under any circumstances for offences against law and order (Article 31). If a diplomat is found to be involved in violence against another person, he may be restrained temporarily, and if necessary, be expelled from the country.

Exemption from Civil Jurisdiction

The exmption from civil jurisdiction is complete so that a diplomat is secured fullest freedom for the peformance of his duties. This immunity, however, does not apply in the case of private business activities of a diplomat. The Vienna Convention of 1961 provides for three exceptions to the immunity of diplomatic agents from civil action, namely: (*a*) A real action relating to private immovable property, unless held on behalf of the sending state; (*b*) action relating to succession to property; and (*c*) action relating to private professional or commercial activity (Article 31). In these specific cases the Vienna Convention permits action against diplomatic agents, provided it does not violate the person of the diplomat. Moreover, diplomats cannot be called at witnesses before a court unless they want to appear voluntarily (Article 31).

Immunity of Official Residence and Premises of the Mission

The residence of a diplomatic agent and of the members of his suite are immune from the control of the local authorities (Article 30). They cannot enter the premises of the mission without the consent of the head of the mission (Article 22). Likewise, the papers, correspondence, messages in code, diplomatic bags and their carriers are also regarded as inviolable and they are entitled to the protection from the receiving state (Article 27). But if a guilty person takes shelter in diplomatic mission, or an individual commits an act within the mission premises which is a crime according to the law of the receiving state, he must be surrendered to that state if such an individual does not enjoy diplomatic immunity or is a domicile of the receiving state. An ambassador, therefore, cannot be allowed to avail himself of the immunity of his house to make it an asylum into which he could admit the criminals and enemies of the state to which he was accredited and defeat the purpose for which he was admitted into that state.

The Right of Asylum in Foreign Missions

The right of asylum in diplomatic mission has been discussed in another chapter. At present the legal position is that the right of diplomatic asylum is not recognised in international law. It is stated in the Vienna Convention on Diplomatic Relations that diplomatic missions are not to be used for the purposes which are incompatible with the discharge of the official duties of such missions.

Exemption from Taxation

The Vienna Convention (1961) provides that a diplomatic agent shall be exempted from all dues and taxes (including sales tax) except certain indirect taxes like sewerage, light and water taxes and taxes on private immovable property in the receiving state which an envoy is expected to pay (Article 34). This exemption is available not only to the head of mission but all the members of the diplomatic staff including family members (Article 37). The diplomats are exempted from personal service of any kind like military service or contributions.

Immunities of an Envoy's Retinue

The dependent relatives of a diplomat living with him and his servants are exempt from civil and criminal jurisdiction of the receiving state. Other officials and servants in a diplomatic mission also enjoy the immunities mentioned above. However, if an individual commits within the mission premises an act which is criminal according to the law of the receiving state he must be surrendered to the authorities of that state, if such an individual does not enjoy the the privilege of extra-territoriality or is the domicile of the receiving state. That means the diplomatic mission cannot consider its premises as its own national territory and apply its own laws to it.

Right of innocent passage through third state Diplomatic agents including their families have a right to innocent passage through the territory of a third state on way to or return from their mission (Article 40). This protection applies to couriers and diplomatic bags as well.

Protection of diplomats. Under the Convention on Protection of Diplomats, any representative or official of a taste or any official or agent of an international organisation is entitled under international law to special protection from any attack on his person, freedom, dignity, as well as members of his family forming a part of his household. Each state party to this convention would regard as a crime under international law the international commission of a murder, kidnapping or any attack upon the person or liberty of an internationally protected person, or a violent attack upon his official premises, private accommodation, or means of transport likely to endanger his person or liberty or a threat to commit such an act. Each state undertakes to punish such crime by appropriate penalty.

In spite of these privileges the envoys are subject to certain restrictions while in the foreign country in the discharge of their duties. They are forbidden by international law to interfere, by word or deed, with the internal political affairs of the local government. They are not allowed to discuss the pending local legislation or controversial questions of party politics. Diplomatic etiquette forbids diplomats to correspond direct with the press upon matters which are the subject of official correspondence between the two countries. Further, a diplomatic embassy cannot be converted into a centre of propaganda and espionage for a foreign state on matters on which the two countries have a dispute. Nor can it be used as an organisation or a refuge of the fifth columnists. The diplomats are agents of goodwill, representing their country at ceremonial functions, and they are supposed to conduct themselves with decorum and dignity. After all, the granting of privileges implies acceptance of a high standard of responsibility and integrity on the part of the diplomat. At times, unfriendly envoys may be subjected to travel restrictions and prevented from visiting certain areas, have their telephones taped and personal effects searched. In contemporary times, unfortunately, the lives of diplomats are not entirely risk free. They have instead become targets of kidnapping, hijacking, bombing, assassination, and other forms of intimidation by insurgent groups.

CONSULAR SERVICE

The history of consular service too dates back to the Greek city-states. It existed even before embassies were established. This service is, therefore, older than the diplomatic service. Their functions pertains to commercial and business relations and to services to nationals living abroad. The specific duties are promotion of trade, settlement of trade disputes, certification of invoices of goods, and enforcement of consular treaties. They have to send detailed reports to home government on economic opportunities, trends of trade, price trends, and canditions of competition. The second function deals with the welfare and where about cases, funeral arrangement, settlement of estates of dead nationals, protection and relief of seamen, notarial seevices and other assistance to their nationals.

Classification of Consular Agents

According to the Vienna Convention of 1963, the consular officers are classified as Consuls-General, Consuls, Vice-Consuls of career, Vice-Consuls not of career, and Consular Agents. The last two are non-career officers.

Consular Rules and Procedures

Consular officers are not diplomatic agents but since they perform certain functions of their state in the foreign territory, they have come to acquire a limited international status and they are governed by treaties or conventions which have now become a part of customary international law. The Vienna Convention of Consular Relations of 1963 which replaced the Havana Convention of 1928 deals with the appointment, functions and the rights and privileges of consuls.

There is much less formality regarding appointment of consular officials. However, their appointments too have to be approved. They receive a commission known as exequatur, which authorises them to discharge their duties as consuls. An exequatur is a sort of an executive order issued by the foreign minister of the receiving state, as a sort of permit which enables him to function in that state.

The Vienna Convention (1963) laysdown the rights and privileges of consuls. It provides that the consular premises and records shall enjoy a certain amount of inviolability (Article 31, 33). The receiving state is required to ensure the freedom of movement and travel in its territory for all consular officers. The consular officers are to be granted freedom of communication for official purposes, and their official correspondence is inviolable (Article 35). Like diplomats, the consular officers are also immune from local civil and criminal proceedings in respect of acts performed in their official capacity. The consular premises and the residence of the consular head are exempt from all dues and taxes other than those for specific services rendered (Article 32). The consular officers are not liable to be arrested and detained pending trial except in cases of grave crime and pursuant to the decision of accompetent judicial authority. Thus consuls enjoy generally as many rights as diplomats, and according to Starke, "the modern tendency of states is to amalgamate their diplomatic and consular services."[3]

Unlike the termination of a diplomatic mission on account of the revolutionary change in the regime of a state or death of a sovereign, the cosular office does not terminate for those reasons. But it may be closed when there is a war between the two countries concerned.

REFERENCES

1. PALMER AND PERKINS, *International Relations*, Calcutta, Scientific Book Agency, 3rd Indian Ed., 1973, p. 85.
2. FENWICK, *International Law*, op. cit., 1971, p. 557.
3. STARKE, *An Introduction to National Law*, op. cit., 1972, p. 394.

Chapter 16

Amicable Methods of Settling International Disputes

In origin the methods of peaceful settlement are very old. The earliest existing treaty dates back to about 3000 B.C. carved in stone. It record the successful arbitration of a boundary dispute between Egyptian kings. The mechanism for peaceful settlement of disputes developed by the Greeks remains unsurpassed till today. Until the end of 12th century there was no provision in international law for peaceful settlement of international disputes. The only legal remedy was resort to arms—war. Of course the method of arbitration was there but it was used sparingly. Jay's Treaty of 1794 marks the beginning of the extensive use of arbitration in modern times. Other land marks are the Hague Conventions of 1899 and 1907 for the Pacific Settlement of International Disputes, the League Covenant, the Statute of the Permanent Court of International Justice, the Geneva Protocol (1924), the General Act for the Pacific Settlement of International Disputes, adopted by the League Assembly in 1928, the Inter-American Arbitration and Conciliation treaties drafted at the Washington Conference (1929), the U.N. Charter and the Statute of the International Court of Justice; the Charter of the Organisation of American States and the Pact of Bogota (1948).

CHIEF METHODS OF PACIFIC SETTLEMENT

Article 1 of the U.N. Charter obliges states to settle their disputes peacefully. Articles from 33 to 38 of the Charter (Chapter 6) deal with the methods of peaceful settlement. The seven methods listed therein are: (1) Negotiation, (2) Good Offices, (3) Mediation, (4) Commission of Enquiry and Conciliation, (5) Arbitration, (6) Judicial Settlement or Adjudication and (7) Resort to Regional Agencies and the United Nations (Article 33). These devices can be divided into two broad categories: one, those based on persuasion with no binding force and two, those having binding character.

1. Negotiation

Negotiation is a legal and orderly administrative process by which governments adjust or settle their differences. Negotiations may be carried on either by heads of state or their agents or by exchange of notes. Some of the well-known examples of successful negotiation are Indo-Pak Agreement on Minorities (1950), Indo-Pak, Indus Water Treaty (1960), Yalta and Potsdam Agreements during Second World War. Most of the international disputes are settled through normal channels of diplomacy. Such machinery is provided both by the OAS and the UN.

2. Good Offices

When a third party offers its services with a view to compose differences between two states who are not willing to negotiate directly, it is said to tender its good offices. In this method, a third party acts as go-between. To illustrate, Kosygin, the Prime Minister of the Soviet Union, played this role admirably at Tashkent between India and Pakistan in 1966. Recently, the Shaat-al-Arab River boundary dispute between Iraq and Iran was resolved (1975) through the good offices of the Algerian President, the late Boumeddin. More recently, Mrs Gandhi offered her good offices and sent G. Parthasarthy to bring round the Tamil leaders to the negotiating table following the July 1983 carnage in Colombo agains Tamils.

3. Mediation

Mediation is conducting of negotiation through the agency of a third party. Mediator may look into the dispute either at his own initiative or at the request of the disputants. The distinction between good offices and mediation it very subtle. The former is different from the latter in the fact that, unlike good offices, the third party itself takes part in the negotiations and suggests terms of settlement.[1] To illustrate, in 1905, President Theodore Rosevelt of America acted as a mediator in the Russo-Japanese war. Switzerland has played this role in a number of disputes. The UN Good Offices Commission for Indonesia (147) performed a notable service in settling disputes between the Dutch Government and the Indonesian Republic after the Second World War, Count Berndotte functioned as a mediator on Jerusalem issue in 1948, Sir Owen Dixon was appointed as a mediator by the UN on the Kashmir issue between India and Pakistan, the Colombo proposals negotiated by 6 Afro-Asian Powers (1963) to settle the Sino-Indian boarder dispute is another example of mediation.

4. Commission of Enquiry and Conciliation

It is a process formulating proposals of settlement after the investigation of facts. The First Hague Conference (1899) favoured Commission of enquiry and the Second Conference (1907) favoured conciliation. The League Assembly also endorsed this method in 1922, and within five years about 52 conciliation treaties were made. The use of commission of enquiry, however, has been negligible. A commission of enquiry has to investigate the facts of a dispute but it largely confines itself to a statement of facts and a clarification of the issues. This technique was employed in the Dogger Bank incident of 1904.[2] In this incident some Russian warships had fired by mistake on the British fishing vessels in the North Sea. The Commission of enquiry provides a cooling off period, while investigation is under way and hostilities are suspended during the enquiry period.

Conciliation differs from Enquiry in that it assumes an obligation on the part of third parties to take initiative in the search for agreement. The distinction between conciliation and mediation is more or less nominal. Mediation is commonly perform by an individual but conciliation by a committee, commission of council. Again, conciliation denotes reference of a dispute to a body of persons for ascertaining facts, but in mediation the initiation comes from the third party. Conciliation is a constructive approach to non-justifiable disputes. In a nutshell, it is a combination of enquiry and mediation.[3] The UN has made a very successful use of such conciliation commissions in dealing with intricate problems such as the Palestine issue, etc. This method is better than Arbitration or Adjudication as it has greater flexibility in comparison to the latter.

5. **Arbitration and Judicial Settlement**

Arbitration is a judicial process. It is different from conciliation in the sense that Conciliation merely recommends solution but Arbitration decides a dispute. The former is a friendly counsel, the letter is a binding decree. On the whole, Arbitration is the most important amicable means. Its value resides in its quasi-judicial character.[4] The methods of Arbitration on disputes is consensual, flexible and efficacious. Judicial Settlement or Adjudication itself is a form of arbitration, in which a permanent court acts as the arbitral tribunal. Arbitration is different from Judicial Settlement in three ways: (*i*) Nomination of arbitrators is made by the parties themselves; (*ii*) Parties themselves select principles or terms of reference upon which the tribunal should base its findings; and lastly, (*iii*) its jurisdiction is voluntary.

The device of Arbitration has been successfully employed throughout the centuries. The procedure was quite common among Greek city states. In modern times the 19th century alone added some 400 examples of successful arbitration, the most famous one being the settlement of the Alabama Claims Controversy[5] (1872). In 1899, however, a Permanent Court of Arbitration was established by the Hague Conference. It was utilized in several cases. It decided about 20 cases between 1900 and 1932. The most famous awards of this Court are the North Atlantic Fisheries case and the Savarkar's Case (1910).

A real advance in the prospects for compulsory jurisdiction was made by the Permanent Court of International Justice and the International Court of Justice. Both these world Courts derive their authority from the same statute and hence the I.C.J. is simply a successor or continuation of the P.C.I.J. The Carnegie Peace Palace at Hague is the seat of the Court. The jurisdiction of the Court comprises all cases which the parties refer to it and all matters specifically provided for in treaties and conventions in force. In general, therefore, the jurisdiction originally conferred was voluntary but in fact the Court has been given a wide compulsory jurisdiction through treaties and conventions in force and through the Optional Clause contained in Article 36 of the Statute. This clause provides that states may of their own accord accept compulsory jurisdiction of the Court in all legal disputes concerning (*a*) the interpretation of a treaty; (*b*) any question of international law; (*c*) the existence of any fact, which, if established, would constitute a breach of international obligation; and (*d*) the nature or extent of reparation to be paid for the breach of an international obligation. By now, about 45 states have accepted the optional clause though in few cases their acceptance is hedged by reservations in areas involving 'vital interests'; matters of 'domestic concern' or 'national honour'.

6. Pacific Settlement and Regional Agencies

The Charter recommends the settlement of disputes by resort to regional agencies of arrangements. All regional systems make elaborate provision for peaceful settlement of disputes among the participating members. For instance, the O.A.S. Charter devotes an entire Chapter on it. In a number of political disputes among American States the O.A.S. has played a very useful intermediary role. The U.N. Charter also provides for this procedure. Article 1 of the Charter emphasises the aspect of settling disputes peacefully. If parties to a dispute fail to settle their conflicts by means indicated in Article 33, they may refer the same to the Security Council under Article 37. That is, when the possibility of Chapter 6 is exhausted the Chapter 7 becomes applicable.

INTERNATIONAL COURT OF JUSTICE

The I.C.J. is an important organ of the United Nations and hence its Statute is annexed to the Charter. All the UN members are automatically parties to the Statute. The Statute is almost a literal copy of the statute of the Permanent Court of International Justice.

Organisation of the Court

The Court consists of fifteen judges whose election requires absolute majority in both the General Assembly and the Security Council. The judges are elected regardless of their nationality from among persons of high moral character, who possess the qualifications required in their respective countries for appointment to the highest judicial offices and are jurists of recognised competence in international law, but there are explicit provisions that no two judges can be nationals of the same state. They are elected for nine years and can be reelected. Incidentally, Dr Nagendra Singh from India was reelected for the second term in 1981. One third of the judges, however, retire after every three years. Article 31 of the Statute permits the judges of the nationality of each of the parties to the dispute to sit in the case before the Court. The judges are given a tax free salary of 3 lakhs a year plus a liberal retirement pension and enjoy diplomatic privileges and immunities.

The seat of the Court is established at Hague but the Court can sit elsewhere as well. The President and Vice-President of the Court are elected by members of the Court from among themselves for 3 years terms and the Registrar resides at the seat of the Court.

Jurisdiction of the Court

The Court has three-fold jurisdiction:

1. **Voluntary jurisdiction**. Article 36 of the Statute of the Court provides that its jurisdiction comprises all cases which the parties refer to it by agreement.

2. **Obligatory jurisdiction**. Para 2 of Article 36 provides that parties to the statute may at any time declare that they recognise as compulsory, ipso-facto and without special agreement, in relation to any other state accepting the same obligation, the jurisdiction of the Court in all legal disputes concerning: (*a*) the interpretation of a treaty; (*b*) any question of international law; (*c*) the existence of any fact, which if established, would constitute a breach of an international obligation; and (*d*) the nature and extent of the reparation to be paid for the breach of an international obligation. The declara-

tion may be made unconditionally or on condition of reciprocity on the part of several or certain states or for a certain time. This declaration provides for compulsory jurisdiction by agreement. The Optional Clause has been accepted by about 45 states by now.

Thus the states cannot be compelled to litigate their dispute before the Court without their own consent. Hence the jurisdiction of the Court is confined to cases which are volutarily submitted to it, except where one of the parties to the dispute has expressly bound itself in advance to accept the jurisdiction of the Court in respect of any particular dispute or class of disputes.

3. **Advisory jurisdiction**. As per Article 65 of the Statute the Court is empowered to give an advisory opinion on any legal question referred to it by the Security Council, the Economic and Social Council and the Trusteeship Council or the General Assembly. Even the UN's Specialised Agencies, when empowered, can seek advisory opinion. Such advisory opinion, however, is not binding upon the parties unless they bind themselves in advance by treaty or agreement with regard to such advice.

Since its existence, the World Court has dealt with more than 60 cases and has handed down 34 judgements and 15 advisory opinions. No doubt, it is a pitiable tally for atribunal of international character. Since the World Court has only optional jurisdiction, few cases are referred to it and hence its docket has been notoriously light.

The decision of this Court include a series of rulings and opinions. The well-known cases are the Coufu Channel dispute between Britain and Albania (1946); Status of South West Africa (1950); dispute between Columbia and Peru over the right of asylum for Victor Haya de la Torre; Anglo-Iranian Oil Dispute (1953); Anglo-Norwegian Fisheries case (1951); India *vs.* Portugal Transit Rights Dispute (1962), a ruling that South Africa's Mandete is illegal (1971), a decision on the dispute among Iceland, West Germany and Britain over the fishing rights of Iceland's Coast (1974); and the advisory opinion on Morocco's claim over the territory of Spanish Sahara (1975).

REFERENCES

1. AKEHURST, MICHAEL, *A Modern Introduction to International Law*, London, George Allen and Unwin, 1970, p. 290.
2. OPPENHEIM, *International Law*, (ed) H. Lauterpacht, Vol. II, 7th Ed. 1952, pp. 11, 13-14.
3. AKEHURST, MICHAEL, *A Modern Introduction to International Law*, p. 291.
4. LAWRENCE, T.J., *Principles of International Law*, (ed.) P.H. Winfield, New York, 1925, pp. 566-67.
5. GREEN, L.C., *International Law through Cases*, op. cit., p. 23.

Chapter 17

Settlement of International Disputes through Non-amicable Means

Failing settlement of international disputes by peaceful means, International Law recognised untill the First World War some coercive non-amicable methods for settling international disputes. After the adoption of the Covenant and the Charter, however, such compulsive methods have not been considered permissible. Under Article 37 read with Article 2 (4) of the Charter parties are obliged to refer their disputes to the Security Council. But since the Security Council can intervene only when a dispute is referred to it the coercive procedures can still the made use of under certain limitations.

International Law thus permits states to adopt non-amicable means with a view to seek redress under certain circumstances and as such they are treated as legitimate methods of self-help. Nevertheless, such coercive methods have to be short of war.

The various forms of such compulsive means are: diplomatic pressure, display of force, retorsion, reprisals, non-intercourse, boycott, embargo, pacific blockade and possible intervention. The possibility that such methods may lead to war can not be ruled out and therefore international law permits them under great restrictions. Since the establishment of the League of Nations and the United Nations these means can be legitimately applied under conditions laid down by the Collective Security system.

1. Retorsion

Retorsion is a retaliatory measure for unfriendly, unjust or discourteous acts. It is a recourse to non-amicable means within the domestic jurisdiction of a state against an unfriendly but not illegal act. The measures adopted are strictly within the legal rights and do not amount to coercion, yet they are indirectly harmful to the other state.

Travel restrictions on the diplomats, recall of ambassadors, withdrawal of fiscal and tariff concessions, depreciation of currency restriction on foreignships, domestic legislation against aliens are some of the ways of retorsion.[1] To illustrate, in 1904, Japan threatended to impose differential duties on Russian imports as the latter excluded Japanese fishermen from Sakhalin waters. Again, India imposed certain disabilities on South-Africans living in India in 1961 and recalled her High Commissioner. Similarly, the Indian diplomat was recalled after the Chinese invasion in 1962. Since such measures do not violate international law the Charter does not disallow this method.

2. Reprisals

Reprisals in peacetime are all the recourse to various hostile measures short of war by one state against illegal acts of another. All coercive measures for the purpose of obtaining redress are called reprisals. They are harmful and otherwise illegal acts of selfhelp performed by one state against another. Though normally illegal, they are rendered legal by a prior illegal act committed by the other state.[2] Reprisals therefore are illegitimate acts validated under certain circumstances. "They are lawful departures from law to compe compliance with law." In other words, "they are deviations from law to develop devotion to law."[3]

Reprisal is the method of putting stress and pressure upon an offending state which is of a violent nature though short of war. Unlike retorsion, it involves an act of international delinquincy. If retorsion is retaliation for misbehaviour, reprisal is a hostile measure for obtaining justice. International law, therefore, permits it in case of denial of justice.

Lawrence divides reprisals into four categories as follows:[4]

(1) *Positive reprisal* means 'tit for tat'. (2) *Negative reprisal* involves refusal to pay a national debt or fulfil a treaty obligation. (3) *Special reprisals* were practised in the Middle Ages underwhich private citizens were authorized by 'letters of marque' to capture vessels and cargoes of the offending nationality. It was a sort of indemnification of private individuals for injuries and losses suffered by them under the authority of the government. This practice lasted till 1763. (4) Under *General reprisal* a state performs warlike operations without the intention of making war such as seizing or destroying property, holding territory or capturing places or vessels.

Measures of reprisal are not confined to actions against states only, e.g., Yugoslavia turned out Hungarians in 1935 consequent on the murder of King Alexander of Yugoslavia at Marsailles. The most notorious case of reprisal was the occupation of Corfu (Greece) in 1923 by Turkey. Another glaring example of reprisal was when America freezed Red Chinese assets and banned trade with the Communist China on her intrusion in Korea and the Peking government inturn seized all American assets like Shanghai Power Company, two oil companies, shipping firms and banks. To cite a recent case, the US Government frezeed Iranian assets by way of reprisal on the hostage issue until (January 1981) they were released. To give a more recent example, India seized a Sri Lankan gunboat (January 1985) after it had killed and intimidated some Indian fishermen in Indian territorial waters. India returned the naval vessel of Sri Lanka along with its seven crews only when Colombo released detained Indian fisherman and trawlers by the end of January 1985.

3. Hostile Embargo

Embargo implies "the detention within the national domain of ships or other property otherwise to find their way to foreign territory." It involves provisional seizure or detention of merchant ships or property of the offending state. In the nineteenth century it was often resorted to in anticipation of hostilities, but if no war followed, the goods seized were released. However, due to growth of commercial interest it is seldom applied these days. Any way, it is a legitimate means if it is not against treaty obligations. The well-known cases of embargo are American Embargo Act of 1807 against Britain and embargo on arms shipment to Mexico from the US in 1912 and more recently, the oil embargo of 1973 adopted by Arab members of the OPEC.

4. Pacific Blockade

Pacific blockade "is an act of force primarily directed against the state blockaded with a view to coercing it to followt he line of policy desired." It is a temporary suspension of commerce by closing access to its coast with no other hostile measurs save to enforce it. It is enforced in peacetime by the navel forces to prevent access to or egress from the ports of another. It is commonly resorted to either (1) by way of reprisals or (2) as a measure of international policy. It is generally adopted by strong navel powers.

Pacific blockade is different from hostile one only in the absence of a formal state of war and in the relations of third states to the blockade. For instance, vessels of third states can be seized if found trying to break it but they cannot be confiscated.

Pacific blockade came to be recognised in the last quarter of the nineteenth century. It was considered legal, if effective, duly notified and maintained by a sufficient force and did not interfere with ships under a foreign flag of third states. The most famous example of pacific blockade was the blockade of Venezuela ports by Britain and Germany in 1902 to settle pecuniary claims. Similarly, in 1916, the

Allied powers blockade Greek Ports in order to prevent Greece from joining forcers with the Central Powers. Again, in 1948 the Soviet Union blockaded West Berlin by closing land routs to West Berlin. The Charter, however, authorizes blockade only on behalf of the United Nations. It is a proper instrument of collective action for enforcing the United Nations' obligations and principles.

5. **Intervention**

Intervention is another compulsive means of settling disputes between states short of war. It is a dictatorial interference by a state in the affairs of another state for the purpose of maintaining or altering the existing order. Intervention may be internal, external, punitive and diplomatic (for detailed discussion see the chapter on Intervention).

It is permissible only for self-defence, enforcement of treaty rights, protection of lives and property of nationals living abroad, but not for the maintenance of balance of power, as earlier. To illustrate, the US intervened in Cuba (1906) under treaty rights and so did France and Britain in the Suez Crisic (1956). But now only the United Nation can legitimately intervene Hence the US intervention in Vietnam (1961-73) and lately in Grenada (1983), the Soviet intervention in Hungary (1956), in Czechoslovakia (1961), in Afganistan (1979) cannot be justified as they are all in violation of Article 2(4) of the Charter and the Resolution No. 2131 passed on 21 December 1965 by the General Assembly, which embodies the declaration on the inadmissibility of intervention in the domestic affairs of other states. The Chapter 7 of the Charter authorizes only the Security Council to resort to collective measures against the defaulting states, such as interruption of economic relations and other communications, severance of diplomatic relations, including blockade for the purpose of preventing breach of peace.

REFERENCES

1. Fenwick, *International Law*, op. cit., 1971, pp. 635-36.
2. Akehurst, Michael, *A Modern Introduction to International Law*, op. cit., p. 15.
3. Mookerjea, Sobhan Lal, *International Law*, Calcutta, A. Mukherjee and Co. Vol. I., Revised 2nd. Ed., 1968, p. 516.
4. Lawrence, in M.P. Tandon, *Public International Law*, op. cit., p. 477.

[illegible] Order' from [illegible] in 19[illegible] [illegible] West Indies [illegible] behalf of the United [illegible] for [illegible]

[illegible]

[illegible] by the [illegible] or alleging the [illegible] relating to [illegible] first [illegible]

[illegible] National [illegible] Vietnam [illegible] question in [illegible] cannot be [illegible] of the Charter [illegible] passed in [illegible] by the General Assembly [illegible] of the [illegible] of other states. The [illegible] Council to [illegible] such as [illegible] purpose [illegible]

[illegible]

[illegible]

PART II

LAW OF WAR AND NEUTRALITY

Chapter 18

War as a Method of Settling Disputes among Nations

Generally understood, "War is the continuation of foreign policy by other means."[1] It is the culmination point in the tactics of foreign policy. It is normally resorted to when other coercive measures are of no avail. But as understood in International Law, War is a contest among different political units by means of armed forces. Quincy Wright defines war as "a violent contact of distinct but similar entities." According to Malinowski, 'it is an armed conflict between two independent political units by means of organised military forces in the pursuit of a national policy." Haffman Nickerson says "War is the use of organised force between two human groups persuing contradictory policies, each group secking to impose its policy upon the other." Lawrance describes war as "a contest carried on by public forces between states with the intention of ending peaceful relations and substituting hostilities for them."[2] According to this definition contest and intention are the two main characteristics of war. To quote Sorensen, a state of war means the absence of peaceful relations, between two or more States, followed by hostilities, if necessary. But at times states may declare a war on each other without engaging in hostilities.[3] The institution of war, although restricted by the Charter, remains still a fact of international life, but it is no more recognised as a legitimate instrument of national policy.

KINDS OF WAR

War differs from other non-amicable modes of settlement such as police action, sanction, blockade, reprisal, intervention, etc. The recognised ways of war are: (1) Total war, (2) Civil war, and (3) Guerilla war.

1. **Total war** The present day war has assumed the character of total war where everything is subordinated to the supreme task of winning the war. It is characterized by its annihilating and unlimited war aims. It is fought by total population for total stakes. All rules, regulations, assurances, treaties and pacts pertaining to war are of no moment. The old distinction of combatants and non-combatants and

military and non-military objectives is no longer recognised. No sanctity is attached to the lives of the civilians. In view of total war, the rules of warfare have become of historical interest only, because in such a war they are not considered to have any validity.

2. **Civil war.** A civil war exists when two parties or groups within a state have recourse to arms for the purpose of obtaining power in the state. The American Civil War (1861-65), the Spanish Civil War (1936-38), the Chinese Civil War (1945-49) are some of the well-known examples of civil war.

3. **Guerilla war.** Guerilla warfare consists in hostilities conducted in territories occupied by the enemy by armed bodies of men who don't form part of an organised army. In other words, it means irregular war secretly carried on by detached, self styled warriors. However, Guerilla wars too are subject to the general war rules as per the Hague Regulations of 1899 and the Geneva Convention of 1949.

EFFECTS OF OUTBREAK OF WAR

The declaration of the outbreak of war has immediate and far reaching effects between the belligerent powers and their subjects:

1. On the outbreak of war, the subjects of the belligerents and their property become endowed with enemy character.

2. Public armed forces of belligerents are invested with the right of starting hostilities.

3. Diplomatic and consular relations are suspended or terminated.

4. All legal relations are suspended and commercial intercourse is declared illegal.

5. No fresh contracts between subjects of belligerents can be allowed and all previous ones are suspended or dissolved. The partnership firms are also dissolved, if the partners acquire enemy character.

6. Through the influence of recent treaties a practice has grown up that debts due to enemy subjects are not annulled but only suspended. It is to be noted that in such a case the limitation does not run against the creditor during the war period.

7. Belligerent property in a natural country is immune from seizure as per rule. But in 1941, the USA froze the assets of Germany and Italy in neutral countries too.

8. Neutral property found in the needy country is not liable to confiscation. It is often frozen. For instance, the US froze the assets of neutral countries over run by Germany while she was still in a state of technical neutrality.

9. According to the old practice all private or public property of

the enemy found within the territory of the belligerent state was liable to seizure and confiscation. But the modern practice forbids the confiscation of private property. However, private property found by the belligerent on his own merchantship is liable to capture.

10. In modern times the enemy subjects are allowed to go out of the country. Those not allowed to leave on security grounds are put under certain restrictions as per Geneva Convention of 1949 on the protection of Civilian Persons in time of war.

11. On occupation of enemy territory during war, the belligerent takes possession of enemy property, whether public or private, for military purposes. The belligerent administers the enemy territory and keeps law and order while respecting, unless absolutery essential, the laws in force in the enemy country as provided in Article 43 of the Hague Regulations.

EFFECTS OF WAR ON TREATIES

The effect of war on treaties is an unsettled issue of international law. Juristic opinions differ widely on this matter. There is one school of thought which maintains that all treaties are put to an end by a subsequent war between two parties. The advocates of this view are Scott, Lord Bathurst, Buchanan, etc. The other school is of the view that some treaties survive the state of belligerency. This view is represented by Wildman, Starke and others.

William Scott contends that "treaties are perishable things and their obligations are dissipiated by the first hostility."[4] Similarily, Bathurst affirms that Britain knows of no exception to the rule that all treaties are put an end to." Buchanan too asserts that "war terminates all treaties subsisting between belligerents." But in the North Atlantic Coast Fisharies Arbitration (1910), it was held that all treaty obligations are not annulled. Hence the truth ties between the two extreme views. As a matter of fact, some treaties are terminated, some remains unaffected and some remain suspended.

According to Starke, there are two tests applicable here—the subjective test and the objective test. Subjectively, the effect of war on a treaty depends upon the intention of the signatories. The objective test is whether it is compatible with the conduct of war.[5] Further, Starke and others also draw a distinction between treaties to which belligerents and others are parties and to which only belligerents are parties. In the first case, law making treaties or Multilateral Conventions such as Declaration of Paris (1856), Genocide Convention (1948), etc., which legislate for the society of nations as a whole are unaffected. Similarly, general conventions on postal and health matters continue.

The treaties contemplating the contingency of war and relating to hostilities come into effect as soon as hostilities start, e.g., the Hague Conventions of 1899 and 1907, the Geneva Convention of 1949 regarding protection of civilians and POWs actually come into operation, as they pertain to war itself.

But treaties to which only belligerents are parties stand on a different footing. Here the position is that some agreements continue. For instance, treaties which set up a permanent state of affairs such as boundary Conventions, neutralization treaties, treaties of cession, lease agreement and recognition of independence are not affected by war, because by their vary nature they are final and not effected by the exigencies of war. But political treaties, such as treaties of alliance and friendship do come to an end. Besides, there are some treaties which are merely suspended during the war. They are the treaties of commerce and extradition. The fate of other treaties depend on the intention of the parties at the time of conclusion of a treaty.

REFERENCES

1. CLAUSEWITZ, KARLVON, *On War*, Trans. by O.J. Mathijs Jolles, New York. Modern Library, 1943, B.K. VIII, p. 596.
2. LAWRENCE, *Principles of International Law*, (ed.), op. cit., p. 309.
3. SORENSEN, M. (ed.) *Manual of Public International Law*, New York, Macmillan, 1968, pp. 804-05.
4. SCOTT, WILLIAM in M.P. Tandon, *Public International Law*, op. cit, p. 489.
5. STARKE, *An Introduction to International Law*, op. cit., 1972, p. 508.

Chapter 19

Enemy Character during War

"Enemy Character is a quality possessed in a greater or less manner by persons and things." However, neither the Hague Conference nor the London Conference could resolve the character controversy of individuals and goods during the war.

ENEMY CHARACTER OF INDIVIDUALS

During war the subjects of the belligerents are endowed with the enemy character. But neutral subjects do not acquire it. The Continental countries adopted the test of nationality while the British and the US practice applied the test of domicile for determining the enemy character of individuals during the war. But since the First World War the Anglo-American view is getting general acceptance as it makes individuals more important than the states, as they identify themselves with the enemy governments and pay taxes to them.

Lawrence categorizes enemy individuals as follows:[1]

1. First in order of importance come persons of armed forces.

2. Then follow the Seamen navigating the merchant vessels; Their position is midway between forces and civilians.

The Hague Convention (1907), however, freed them, if they promised not to involve themselves in war.

3. Next come persons who follow the army of the enemy without directly belonging to it. They include correspondents, reporters, contractors, etc. When detained, they are to be tried as prisoners of war.

4. Persons domiciled in enemy country, even though neutral by nationality, in case they continue to remain there after the declaration of war. It depends upon their intention to live at a certain place for long.

5. Persons domiciled in a neutral country having houses of trade in enemy country acquire enemy character. This exempts the enemy nationals if they reside and trade in a neutral country.

At the outbreak of war belligerents permit enemy subjects to depart. England did so during the two world wars. But Germany did not. It is a rule that nationals of a state not taking part are neutrals.

But if they render unneutral service, or domiciled in the enemy country and thereby contribute to war, are treated as enemies. The English Trading with the Enemy Act (1939) defined enemy with regard to individuals as any individual residing in enemy territory. Yet the King's Bench Division declared Alfred Liebmann as alien (though he had 26 years residence in England), as he was a natural born German. In this exceptional case the test of alleginance rather than domicile was applied by the Court. The American Trading with the Enemy Act (1917) applied 2 tests: (*a*) any individual partnership residing in enemy nation at war with the US, and (*b*) the government of any nation at war with the US.

ENEMY VESSELS

The character of a vessel is determined prima faeie by the flag it flies. The Declaration of London (1909) confirmed this customary rule of international law. According to Lawrence, a ship charactered by the enemy or navigated by an enemy captain and crew would be treated as enemy property, even though she belonged to a neutral power and the same fate would be meted out to neutral ships if flying enemy flag. But the defect of London Declaration came to light during the First World War, and hence, in 1915, British and French Governments substituted a new rule in place of Article 57 of the London Declaration: "that the enemy or neutral character of ships depended upon the nationality of owners rather than the flag." This was done as certain ship owners in the US, who in order to circumvent the effect of the declaration, purchased with German capital and operated under the US flag a number of merchant vessels while America was still a neutral.

The general rule (flag rule), therefore, is now governed by certain exceptions:

1. Enemy owned vessels sailing under neutral flag acquire enemy character if found engaged in carrying military persons or despatches concurrently with other employment of an innocent character.
2. Neutral merchantmen acquire enemy character: (*a*) if they take direct part in the hostilities; (*b*) if they are under the order or control of an enemy agent; (*c*) if they are in the exclusive employment of the enemy; and (*d*) if they are being exclusively appropriated by the enemy for his own purposes.
3. Enemy owned vessels flying a neutral flag or neutral merchant-

men acquire enemy character, if they resist legitimate exercise of right of visit and search or capture.

Transfer of Ships during the War

A wide cleavage exists between the British and the US practice on the one hand and the French and the Russian view on the other regarding transfer of vessels to neutral registry to avoid capture. The former allowed it, if the transfer was bonafide without any reservation even after the outbreak of war. The latter claimed the right of capture, if transfer took place after the outbreak of war. According to French practice, if the transfer was made with reservation while in transit or in blockaded port it was invalid. Regarding transfer of ships Articles 55 and 56 of the Declaration (1909) say: (1) transfer before the outbreak of war is valid unless it is proved that it was made to avoid capture and (2) transfer after the outbreak of war is valid if the owner proves that it was not done to avoid capture. These rules, however, apply to private enemy ships only.

Transfer of Goods at Sea

The Anglo-American practice refuses to recognise transfer of goods at sea after the start of hostilities. But France does recognise it, if it is bonafide transfer.

Under the Hague Convention of 1907 if a merchant ship of a neutral is found in an enemy port, it would be allowed to depart freely. If the ship is unable to leave within the contemplated period, it could be detained but was not to be confiscated. If it is ignorant of the existence of hostility it could be detained and restored without indemnity or destroyed on payment of compensation.

Character of Cargoes

Great controversy persists regarding the character of cargoes on enemy vessels. On the continent, France, Germany, Italy and others regarded the nationality of owners as the test irrespective of domicile. Britain, US, Japan and Holland made the domicile of the owner the test of enemy or neutral character of Cargoes. According to the British and American view, if the owners were domiciled in a neutral country although of enemy nationality, their property was not to be deemed as enemy property. Likewise, if a neutral does business in enemy country his goods get enemy character.

The London Naval Conference (1909) could not reconcile these conflicting views. It merely laid down: "the neutral or enemy character of goods found on board an enemy vessel is determined by the neutral or enemy character of the owner and threreby left the question open.

Neutral Goods on Belligerent Merchant Ships and Vice Versa

Following Consolato del Mare (Maritime Code of Middle Ages) Britain made the ownership of goods the test of liability to capture. The US followed it, except under a treaty to the contrary. They both regarded neutral goods as not liable to capture. The Declaration of Paris (1856) finally settled it providing that (1) the neutral flag covered enemy goods with the exception of contraband of war and (2) the neutral goods under enemy flags are not liable to capture except the contraband of war. Though originally only seven powers signed this Declaration even non-signatories subsequently observed it.

But now "by the extension of the term contraband to cover all commodities of use direct or indirect in war, by the extension of the doctrine of continuous voyage, and by the presumption of hostile destination, the rule that the neutral flag covers enemy goods except contraband of war, has been almost nullified", as Pitt Cobbet has observed.

Enemy Property

All enemy state or public property such as armed vessels, guns and funds can be acquired except works of art or other property unconnected with war. On land the property of enemy subjects is exempt from capture except under special conditions. There is generally required a legislative enactment to authorize such condemnation of private property. Belligerenet property in a neutral state is immune. Germany, therefore, kept her loot in Sweden and Switzerland, but the allied powers had agreement with the latter to seize the same and Britain was appointed the custodian of enemy property. But such measures are contrary to law although the US also froze the assets of Germany, Italy in 1941 after joining the war.

Corporation

The enemy character of corporation is determined by the principle of domicile. The guiding factor is the domicile of the persons who control the destinise of the company.[2] Enemy character it attached to companies as to where they are incorporated, even if the territory is under hostile occupation.

In the well-known case of Daimler Co. Ltd. *vs.* Continental Tyre and Rubber Co.,[3] the latter claimed to recover a sum of money from the former. Lord Parker held that no action lay, as the Company (Continental Tyre and Rubber Company), though registered in

London (1905), was carrying on business in Germany and its agents or de facto control was with those who resided in an enemy state. The character of individual shareholders was immaterial. This judgement thus laid down 2 tests: (1) Incorporation and (2) The place of business for determining the enemy character of corporation. Incapacity of an Alien Enemy in English Law.

A British subject is an alien enemy, if he resides and does business in an enemy country in war times. Likewise, an alien enemy is an alien friend, if he resides and does business in England. Further, an alien enemy can't sue in England during war time but he can be sued for any claim.

Effect of Occupation on Nationality

Occupation not followed by conquest does not involve any complete change of nationality of local citizens, as the transfer of authority is only temporary.

REFERENCES

1. LAWRENCE, (ed), *Principles of International Law*, op. cit., pp. 345-59.
2. COBBET, PITT, *Leading Cases on International Law*, Vol. II, 5th Ed., p. 40.
3. (1916) 2 A.C., p. 307.

Chapter 20

War Crimes and Nuremberg Trial

War crime presents a great difficulty, for every violation of law of war is not a war crime. The term 'war crime' is used here in a technical or juristic sense and not moral.

Oppenheim writes, "war crimes are such hostile and other acts of soldiers or other individuals as may be punished by the enemy on capture of the offenders." He classifies them as follows:[1]

1. Violation of recognised rules of warfare committed by members of armed forces. It includes use of poisonous gases, killing of wounded or surrendered persons, ill-treatment of POWs, killing of hostages, torture of civilians, wanton destruction of museum, hospitals, etc.
2. All hostilities in arms committed by non-members.
3. Espionage, seboteurs and war treason.
4. Maraudings—This is done by those who have left the army yet follow it and indulge in illegitimate warfare, killing wounded persons, and doing acts of robbery and pillage.

To these four categories of crime two more were added by the Nuremberg Tribunal (1946).

5. Crimes against peace—it includes (*i*) planning, preparation, initiation or waging of war of aggression or war in violation of international agreements or treaties and (*ii*) participation in the common plan or conspiracy of the accomplishment of any acts mentioned above.
6. Crimes against humanity—it includes crimes such as large scale massacre, persecution of race (genocide), enslavement, deportation of civilian population, etc.

It is worth mentioning here that the UN General Assembly adopted in 1969 a Convention on the non-applicability of statutory limitations to war crimes and crimes against huminity. Its implication is that there is no time limitation for taking action against such crimes. The Convention came into force on November 11, 1970. In 1973, the Assembly adopted an international Convention on the Suppression and punishment of the Crime of Apartheid and hence these crimes are punishable under International Law.

NUREMBERG TRIAL

Its Genesis. At the Moscow Conference (1943) the 3 Great Powers declared to punish German war criminals. The Yalta Conference (1945) reiterated it. Subsequently the UN constituted a War Crimes Commission under the leadership of Lord Wright to draw up lists of criminals. A Charter was also drawn up by the prosecutors of the 4 Allied powers. In 1945, the London Agreement of Big Four decided to try major war criminals of European Axis whose offences had no particular geographical location. To this Agreement was attached the Charter establishing an International Military Tribunal consisting of the British, French, Russian and American members. Article 6 of this Charter defind the crimes within the jurisdiction of the Tribunal and for which there was individual responsibility such as crimes against peace, crimes against huminity and war crimes.

The hearing of this trial began on November 20, 1945 and ended on August 31, 1946. Twenty-four of the principal Nazi Offenders were indicated as major war criminals before the Tribunal on four counts.[2] The judgement was delivered on October 1, 1946. Out of 22 leaders (2 escaped) of Third Reich of Germany, 12 were sentenced to death, 3 to life imprisonment, only 3 were acquitted and 4 to various terms.

Defence Arguments

1. It was submitted that expost facto punishment is abhorrent to all law. There can be no punishment without pre-existing law. But in this case this principal was violated.
2. That aggression was not a crime. There was no statute to define it (only in 1974 a definition was made available) and no penalty or court to try and punish it.
3. That the defendants were not personally responsible for the crimes. The plea of superior order was an additional argument.
4. That only act of state and not those of individuals are covered under international law. Their plea was that their action should be treated as an "act of state".

Observations of the Tribunal

The maxim that there can be no punishment without a pre-existing law did not apply to present facts. This principle was not a limitation on sovereignty but was only a general principle of justice. Further, the punishment given was not unjust. In addition, the defendants had knowingly violated certain treaties. Further, the Paris Pact (1928) was binding on them, as Germany was a signatory to the Pact.

Again, the fact that the defendants acted pursuent to orders of his government or a superior should not free them from personal responsibility but they may be considered in mitigation of the punishment, for the true test is not the existence of order but whether moral choice was possible. The executioners of a plan are, therefore, not absolved of responsibility. Besides, to initiate a war of aggression was a supereme international crime and for this the representatives of state could not be protected if found guilty, for "crimes are committed by men, not by abstract entities" and it is only by punishing them that the provisions of international law can be enforced. The Charter, therefore, was not arbitrary but an expression of the existing international law.

CRITICISM OF THE TRIAL

Firstly, the military tribunal was established by the victors and it did not include any German or neutral Judges and hence it violated the principle of impartiality. Secondly, too much reliance was placed on the Paris Pact of 1928. No doubt the Pact did outlaw war as an instrument of national policy but it said nothing about personal responsibility. No doubt, war was an offence according to the Pact but not a crime. The words of the Pact were not those of a penal statute; they were the language of theology and not of law. Though the Pact declared aggressive war as illegal but it was no international crime so as to make individuals liable. Besides, the Pact was broken earlier by Japan (1932), Italy (1935), and Germany (1938) also but its violation was not agitated against. It was dug out from the lumber room only when found convenient to victors.

Prof. Schick in his 'The Nuremburg Trial' entertains doubt about the legality of the Charter of the Tribunal. The court of victors was not a proper tribunal. It excluded any German Judge or even a neutral Judge.[3] Again, the Charter was applied with retrospcetive effect. It was a Post-crime law. To Professor Smith, it violates the fundamental principal of impartiality. Both the Tribunal and its laws were the product of the Charter, which was an executive agreement. Kelsen (a German jurist) treast the London Agreement (1945) establishing individual criminal responsibility as expost facto law, and thereby had a retroactive character. But accusation of retroactive legislation was closer to truth as regards crimes against peace and humanity only. A number of treaties and resolutions of 1920s did exist as evidence of international law declaring aggression as illegal. Kelsen also adds that the German sovereign state was subjected to foreign jurisdiction without consent. No doubt, the trial was clearly one sided. The atrocities of Germans were only a question of degree. Had not the Russians did the same in 1939?

The comments of Corbett is comparatively more balanced. He observes: "that the proceedings, admirable as they were in tone and guided as they were by a genuine effort to spare the innocent and to equate punishment with offence, did not amount to adjudication properly so called. The structure of the Tribunal, its terms of reference and the circumstances in which it sat excluded the objective guarantee of impartiality that characteries strict adjudication. There continues to be grave doubts as to the legal character of the principles which it involved."[4]

TOKYO TRIAL (1946-48)

The trial of 26 Japanese major war criminals was started in June 1946 in Tokyo upon the same general principles on which the earlier trial took place. The Tribunal consisted of 11 Judges presided by an Australian Judge. While the tribunal in its judgement on November 4, 1948 found the defendants guilty, Dr Radha Benod Pal, who represented India on the Tokyo Tribunal, gave a dissenting judgement. According to Dr Pal, war in international life remained outside the province of law and that the Paris Pact was not a law. Further no customary law had develop to make war a crime. He held that whatever Tojo and his group did was out of patriotic motive and, therefore, they could not be changed with conspiracy, which was not a crime in international law. He therefore found none of them guilty.

Significance of Nuremberg Trial

It was customary before the First World War to insert a clause in Peace treaties allowing immunity to all persons who have committed wrongful acts. The Versailles Treaty (1919) for the first time inserted a clause providing for the trial of Kaisar William II for a supereme offence against international morality and sanctity of treaties under the provision of Article 227. But the attempt was foiled, as Holland had refused to surrender him for the purpose. The Nuremberg trial was thus a unique event in international affairs in the sense that it has set up a new precedents in the history of internanational law. The plea of respondent superior will not in future relieve a subordinate of his own responsibility as an individual in international law.[5] It has therefore considerably widened its scope. Although the trial had little juristic plane to stand upon, its significance cannot be underestimated. It was an embryo of a real international tribunal for trying aggression. It was on the precedence of this trial that Bangladesh could think of trying 195 Pakistani war leaders.

At least, after Nuremberg there can be no pleas or complaints of retroactive legislation. Its principles are now endorsed by the General Assembly of the United Nations and approved by the International Law Commissioner.

The International Law Commission has formulated seven principles of Nuremberg which are as follows:

1. Any person committing a crime under international law is liable to punishment.
2. Where internal/domestic law does not impose a penalty, an offender will not be relieved under international law. This implies the supremacy of international law.
3. The Heads of State and Responsible Government Officials cannot be absolved from personal responsibility.
4. The fact of superior order did not relieve an offender provided a moral choice was avilable to him.
5. Any person charged with a crime under international law has the right to a fair trial on the fact as well as law.
6. The crimes against Peace, War Crimes and Crimes against Humanity are punishable.
7. Complicity in the commission of such crime is also punishable under international law.

GENEVA CONVENTION OF 1949

The ruthless atrocities committed by the Nazi Germany during Second World War necessitated a revision of the Hague Regulations and other Conventions dealing with rules of warfare and this resulted in the adoption of the Geneva Convention of 1949.

In August 1949, about fifty-eight states of the world assembled at Geneva and signed a Charter for the protection of soldiers as well as civilians in War. Four Conventions were attached to this Charter:

I. Convention on humane treatment of the wounded, the sick and the dead. It enjoins the Government capturing the sick and wounded soldiers to feed and clothe them and treat them in these respects on a level with its own troops. The belligerent must submit death certificates and arrange for the transmission of their belonging to their guardians.

II. Convention on the protection of the soldiers in the sea. It lays down rules for the treatment of the sick, the wounded and the shipwrecked in naval warfare. Military hospitalships, medical transport and medical aircrafts enjoy immunity from capture and other kinds of molestation. It is provided that neutral warships or military aircrafts shall be used to carry shipwrecked persons.

III. Convention on the protection of the prisoners of war.

IV. Convention on the protection of noncombatant civilians and their residence in occupied areas. It expressly prohibits looting and acts of violance, destruction of civilians' property except on military grounds. It enjoins upon the belligerent to provide safety of women, children and old people and to provide food and medical services for the population. Further, it disallows forcible transfer of civilians. Again, no pressure aiming at securing enlistment in the army is permitted. The penal laws of the occupied territory shall continue unless they constitute a threat to security. New penal laws, if any, should be well notified. The occupying State is under an obligation to maintain the former courts. It cannot take hostages or impose collective penalties against the population for breaches of security by the individual inhabitants. It cannot compel pople to give information. Inhabitants of the occupied territory are punishable with death penalties only when they are proved guilty of espionage and of serious acts of sabotage. Civilians accused of offences during occupation are entitled to a regular trial and to a right of appeal.

Recently a resolution was adopted by 139-Nation Conference (1977) to revise the Geneva Convention of 1949. It prohibits the bombing of dams dykes, nuclear power plants, starvation and civilian and attacks on food supplies, crops, livestocks, drinking water sources, and irrigation works as a method of warfare or act of reprisal.

It is worth mentioning here that Article 3 of each of the four Conventions extend some basic laws of war to all civil wars regardless of recognition of belligerency.

Geneva Convention of 1949 and Prisoners of War

The Convention on the protection of the prisoners of war is regarded as the most important of all the four Conventions. Article 4 of this Convention lays down the following categories of prisoners of war to whom the terms and conditions of the Convention would be applicable:

1. Members of the regular armed forces of the belligerent and any other volunteer corps forming part of such forces.

2. Members of other militias of a belligerent working outside its territory, as well as guerilla warriors, if they are properly commanded, bear arms openly, carry distinctivc sign, and obey the laws of war as recognised by international law. A recent Interntional Conference (1977) extended this Convention to benefit guerilla armies also.
3. Members of the regular armed forces professing allegiance to government and authority not recognised by the detaining power.
4. Civilians accompanying army, like correspondents, supply contractors and journalists duly authorised by the belligerent army. Now by a resolution of 139-Nation Conference (1977), the rights in favour of POWs are extended to all journalists covering areas of conflict.
5. Crew, including civilians, engaged in the aircrafts and ships of the belligerent.
6. Inhabitants of a non-occupied territory, resisting the invaders, if they obey the laws of war.

It is further provided that even when there would be doubts as regards the status of a prisoner of war he would not be deprived of the benefits of the Convention. However, bands of marauders without command, deserters captured among enemy troops, enemy spies, even if belong to Army, cannot claim protection. They are liable to be executed.

Besides, Article 13 seeks to guarantee honourable and humane treatment of POWs. There would be no reprisals in respect of them. They would be treated with due consideration of their personal safety, their sex and their honour. They would retain their full 'civil capacity' during detention period. Article 15 provides for free medical treatment and other allied facilities to them. Moreovers, the detaining power cannot seek any information from a prisoner by torture. Besides, their personal belongings cannot be snatched away. Article 19 declares that POWs could be evacuated by the detaining power to a safer zone and they would be kept in a healthy place and provided with the fullest freedom, including religious freedom. Further, officers cannot be made to work, only non-officers can be asked to work but they will be paid for it.

Thus the Geneva Convention of 1949 contains an elaborate programme of rights and privileges of prisoners of war. It takes due note of the fundamental individuality in respect of each war victim as an honourable human being.

The 'Panmunjon agreement' of 1953 made at conclusion of the

Korean war stipulated some important provisions as to the treatment of POWs of the Korean war. Firstly, it provide for screaning of prisoners by a neutral authority. Secondly, before a choice indicated by a prisoner is taken to be final, he should be removed to the control of a neutral authority. Finally, if prisoners refuse to go home, they can go to a neutral country if they are offered permanent home there.

REFERENCES

1. Oppenheim in M.P. Tandon, *Public International Law*, op. cit., p.540.
2. Mahajan, V.D., *Public International Law*, op. cit., Vol. II, pp. 642-46.
3. Prof. Schick in M.P. Tondon, *Public International Law*, op. cit., p. 544.
4. Corbett, P.E., *Law and Society in the Relations of States*, p. 236.
5. Sorensen, M. (Ed.), *Manual of Public International Law*, op. cit., p. 518.

Chapter 21

The Law of Neutrality

In the words of Oppenheim, "neutrality is the attitude of impartiality adopted by third states towards belligerents and recognised by the belligerents, such attitude creating rights and duties between the neutral states and the belligerents."[1] Lawrence defines neutrality as "the condition of those states which in time of war take no part in the contest but continue pacific intercourse with the belligerents."[2] To quote Starke. "In its technical sense, it is a legal status involving a complex of rights, duties and privileges at international law which must be respected by belligerents and neutrals alike."[3]

FEATURES OF NEUTRALITY

The attitude of neutrality does not connote passive impartiality or inactivity but affords rights to a neutral state to protect its frontiers or defend itself when her rights are violated. But at the same time it obliges the neutral states to observe certain duties prescribed by customary law or international conventions. The question of neutrality, however, arises when there is war. That is, neutrality is an incident of war. Moreover, neutrality has to be recognised by belligerents. A neutral state can continue its relation with belligerents and can carry on humanitarian work. It can also intervene if a belligerent violates rules of neutrality.

KINDS OF NEUTRALITY

Neutrality may be perfect or imperfect. It may be temporary or permanent. Again, it may be general, partial, voluntary and conventional. It may also be armed neutrality or benevolent neutrality.

Neutrality, however, is different from neutralization, for whereas neutrality is temporary, particular and voluntary, neutralization is permanent, general and involuntary. Switzerland, Sweden, Finland, Malta, and Austria are some of the models of permanent neutrality. The three fundamental pillars of permanant neutrality are: A state has to bind itself (*a*) to declare its permanent neutrality and to resolve to maintain and defend it with all the means at its disposal; (*b*) never to join in any military alliance or permit the establishment of military bases by foreign states on its territory, and (*c*) never to participate in a war between other states.

Neutrality in war should not be confused with 'neutrality' or 'neutralism' used in the political sense. The latter means non-participation in alliances, or not joining blocs. Again, neutrality is not the same as nonalignment which implies independence of action in national interest and keeping away from military blocs. Neutralism, like nonaligment, is something more than an attitude or a policy; it is a philosophy of foreign policy. Further, it is more political than legal. Connected more with International Relations than International Law."[4]

Rise and Fall of Neutrality

The term 'neutrality' was unknown in the early stages of international law. As an institution of international law neutrality developed gradually during the 17th century. It was about 1648 that people began to speak or write of neutrality. Even Grotius gave little room to it in his works. The principles and practices of neutrality were developed in the 17th and 18th centries. Vattel and Bynkershoek were great writers on neutrality. The idea of neutrality gained momentum with the development of trade and improved means of communication and it became necessary to prevent war from affecting smooth operation of neutral trade and commerce. During the American War of Independence Russia proclaimed the First Armed Neutrality Act in 1780 and declared that neutral vessels should be allowed to navigate from port to port of belligerents. The US adopted this attitude at the outbreak of war between England and France in 1793 and passed the First Neutrality Act in 1794. Russia proclaimed a Second Armed Neutrality Act in 1800 against British refusal to concede immunity from visit and search to neutral merchantmen under convoy.

The concept of neutrality developed in the 19th century along its classical concept of strict impartiality. It was influenced mostly by 3 developments: (*i*) the US attitude in Napoleonic War, (*ii*) permanent neutralization of Switzerland (1815), Belgium (1839) and Luxemburg (1867) obligating them to a neutral attitude, and (*iii*) the Declaration of Paris stipulating the rule that neutral goods on enemy ship must not be appropriated and neutralship covers enemy goods except the contraband of war.

The Second Hague Conference (1907) contained two conventions on neutrality. Convention-V conferred duties and rights of neutrals in wars on land and Convention-XIII conferred rights and duties in naval wars.

The next development took place in the law of neutrality as a result of London Declaration (1909). This Declaration concerns the laws of naval war comprising blockade, contraband, unneutral service, destruction of neutral prizes, transfer of neutral ships, enemy character, visit and search and other matters. This Declaration, however, remained unratified when the First World War started. Any way, it has brought most important changes in the concept of neutrality. To take a few provisions of the London Declaration, it is provided that a neutral vessels if captured was not to be destroyed (Article 48). It is also provided that the transfer by belligerents of their vessels to a neutral flag was void if transfer was made during a voyage or in a blockaded port (Article 56). Article 57 states that the neutral character of vessel was determined by the flag which it was entitled to fly while the status of goods on board an enemy vessel was determined by the character of its owner.

Impartial neutrality, however, had a short run. The First World War gave it short shrift. The traditional neutrality yielded place to a policy of taking sides. During this war neutrality law broke down. No wonder, it prompted Wilson to declare that "neutrality is no more possible in fact and no more desirable in law."

Neutrality and the League Covenant

The Covenant of the League of nations envisaged two kinds of war: (1) not in disregard of the League obligations and (2) in disregard of the League obligation. In the former case, the Covenant left nations free to remain neutral in the traditional sense but it greately affected the law of neutrality in the second case. Article 16 states: "If any war is resorted to against the Covenant, it is an act of war against all other members and they must apply both economic and military sanctions. Obviously, the inclusion of such measures under the collective security system amounted to an abandonment of the attitude of absolute impartiality and violation of neutrality. The collective security system implies that a war anywhere against anyone is a war against everyone and everywhere. Fenwick, therefore, observes that Article 16 puts and end to the traditional view of neutrality. Kelsen, likewise, commented that the enforcement of economic and military sanctions was inconsistent with the obligations of a neutral state. Oppenheim, however, takes a balanced view when he says: "where resort to war was not contrary to the Covenant, the law of neutrality was not affected." He added that without abolishing neutrality, the Covenant had vitally affected it in those cases in which members of the League were bound to apply sanctions under Article 16 of the Covenant. According to Philip Jessup, neutrality was still possible in spite of the Covenant.

Subsequently, the General Treaty for the Renunciation of War (1928) brought about a fundamental change in the status of war and hence also that of neutrality, because war as a right of sovereign state was renounced as an instrument of national policy. But within few years the system of collective security received a jolt by the Second World War. The out-break of World War II witnessed gross violation by Germany of the neutrality of Norway, Denmark, Holland, Belgium and Luxemburg in 1940 and had a far-reaching effect on the neutral states of America. In 1940, the US agreed to transfer Britain 50 old destroyers in exchange for the right to lease naval and air bases in certain countries.

The experience of the Second World War has thus shown that the traditional law of neutrality has become obsolete. The modern war is a total war in which military and economic aspects are inextricably mixed and a belligerent is not in a position to make traditional concession to neutrals. In total war complete isolation is impossible and absolute neutrality cannot be maintained. It is testified by the fact that even the champion of neutrality (USA) could not remain neutral during the Second World War.

Neutrality and the U.N. Charter

The position of neutrality under the Charter almost resembles to what was under the Covenant. Article 2(5) imposes obligation on all members to give every assistance in any action the UN takes and to refrain from giving any assistance to any state against which it is taking preventive or enforcement action. Under Article 25 the UN members have agreed to accept and carry out the decisions of the Security Council. A whole chapter (7) from Article 39 to 51 relates to action with respect to threats to peace, breaches of peace and acts of aggression. Article 41 obliges the UN members, if the Security Council so requires, to severe economic, diplomatic and commercial relations with the guilty states. Under Articles 42 and 43 the Security Council may require members to take Armed action against such states. In other words, the members are required to contribute according to agreement armed forces, assistance and facilities for maintaining international peace and security. Finally, Article 51 permits even neutrals to take part in individual and collective self-defence in the wake of an armed attack against a member of the United

Nations.

No doubt, these provisions in the Charter leave no room for neutrality as a legal system. However, there can be envisaged situations in which the Security Council may not take enforcement action against the guilty in the absence of the required majority on account of Veto. In such a case there is no legal obligations on members to relinquish their neutrality. The Geneva Convention of 1949 itself refers to neutral countries when providing for protection to war victims. Further more, some of the post-1945 armistic agree ments bestow supervisory powers on neutral country.

A number of writers have expressed their opinion on the position of neutrality under the Charter. For instance, Kelsen states: "according to one interpretation, the rule of international law imposing the obligation of impartiality upon neutral states is superseded by the Charter."[5] According to Fenwick, the adoption of the Charter marks the end of neutrality as a legal system. To quote Morgenthau, "the UN did not kill neutrality but rather sentenced it to die staying indefinitely the execution of the sentence." In the opinion of Oppenheim, "though affected it, the Charter has not substantially abolished the right to neutrality."

The consensus of opinion among writers is that in principle, no member is entitled to remain neutral in a war in which the Security Council takes action.[6] But the example of Korean action shows that in practical effect the legal consequences do not follow necessarily. In spite of the Security Council Resolution on June 27, 1950, only 16 nations sent arms for the Korean action. Sharing the view of Lauterpacht one can say that the Charter has affected the right of neutrality in a decisive way but not substantially abolished the right to remain neutral."

A complex of factors have weakened the validity of the view that neutrality is not permissible under the Charter. For instance, Article 27 (3) of the Charter provides that the decision of the Security Council requires a majority of votes, including the concurring votes of all the 5 permanent members for collective action against a permanent member. It is absurd to expect concurrence on the part of that permanent member with such action. As such it permits a state to remain neutral. No agreement has been concluded so far to take collective action as provided under Article. 43.

To conclude, "the laws of neutrality have undoubtedly suffered two massive blows in the present century: (1) the coming of total war and (2) the introduction of Collective Security system in international relations. As a result, neutrality can have no meaning either in fact or in law."[7] As a matter of fact, "neutrality is a fair weather vessel; the storm of a total war makes a wreck of it."

REFERENCES

1. OPPENHEIM, *International Law*, Lauterpacht (ed.), Vol. II, 1966 p. 653.
2. LAWRENCE, *The Principles of International Law*, op. cit., p. 582
3. STARKE, *An Introduction to Intrrnational Law*, op. cit., 1972, p. 534.
4. MOOKERJEA, SOBHAN LAL, *International Law*, op. cit, pp, 534-35.
5. KELSEN, HANS, *Principles of International Law*, (ed) R.N. Tucker, New York, Rinehart and Winston, 1966, p. 87.
6. OPPENHEIM, *International Law*, op. cit., Vol II, 7th ed., p. 647.
7. SVARLIEN, *Introduction to the Law of Nations*, p. 373.

Chapter 22

Rights and Duties of Neutral States

The rights of neutral states correlate to the duties of the belligerents in their dealings with each other. Likewise, the duties of neutrals correspond to the rights of belligerents. Oppenheim mentions impartiality and acquiescence as summarising both the rights and duties of the neutrals. But Lawrence gives an exhaustive enumeration of the rights and duties of neutrals as follows:

RIGHTS OF NEUTRAL STATE

1. Inviolability of neutral territory. This is the most important right and is stated in the Hague Conventions V and VIII of 1907. These Coventions admit the rights of neutrals to resist with force any voilation of its territory. To take an example, in 1807, Britain destroyed a Danish Fleet as her integrity was indanger. Similarity, the US captured a German ship (*Florida*) in Brazilian territorial waters during the First World War. During this very War Holland, a neutral state, fired upon a belligerent air-planes violating the Dutch airspace. Although it is the duty of the belligerent to treat neutrals in accordance with the observance of impartiality by neutrals, this duty excludes any violation of neutral territory for military purposes and the interference with the legitimate commercial intercourse with the enemy.

2. To have its territory immune from hostile activities. The Hague Convention (1907), however, justifies a temporary violation in case of extreme necessity but of course with an explanation to the neutral. Referring to 'Caroline' Lawrence points out that such a temporary viotation under the stress of a great emergency should be taken as a technical offence and should not be regarded as serious wrong so as to claim substantial reparation.

3. To have its territory immune from direct preparation for act of hostilities. The Hague Convention says that no warlike expedition is to be fitted and that it should not be used as a base of operation.

4. To continue diplomatic intercourse with either belligerent.

5. Right to recognise a de fecto belligerent. For example, Britain recognised the Franco regime as de fecto belligerent in the Spanish

Civil War of 1936-38.

6. To have its submarine cable connecting a belligerent territory unmolested subject to the right of self preservation of belligerent. In case the connection is cut by the action of belligerent it has to be restored and compensation to be paid.

7. To have regulation made for the protection of neutrality obeyed by the belligerent. Only sick and wounded or those driven by the enemy can come across its prontiers. In sea warfare, belligerent warships freely enjoy the hospitality of its ports and waters.

8. To refuse passage to belligerent troops across the country.

9. To grant asylum to belligerent forces.

10. To claim reparation from any belligerent state which violates its neutrality. International rules, however, only prescribe the scale on which indemnities should be calculated. It shoule be adequate and in proportion to the gravity of the offence.

11. To protect its citizens living in belligerent states. Generally they are withdrawn otherwise they will have to pay war tax and suffer from some restrictions. But they cannot be drafted forcibly into the belligerents' army.

12. Right to purchase belligerent vessels before the outbreak of actual war.

13. To maintain its exclusive jurisdiction over its territory. Hence no prize court can be established by the belligerent on its territory.

14. Right to freedom of commerce. A neutural state has right to the freedom of commerce with either of the belligerents. The Declaration of Paris (1856) stipulates that neutral goods on enemy ships are not liable to capture and enemy goods were covered by neutral flag except the contraband of war. In other words, non-contraband commerce is allowed with both the belligerents.

15. Right to postal correspondence. The Hague Convention XI provided that postal correspondence (not parcels) of neutrals or belligerent found on a neutal or enemy vessels at sea was inviolate. However, these rules were nor observed during the two world wars.

DUTIES OF NEUTRAL STATES

Obviously, the duties of neutrals are correlative to the rights of belligerents. They may be summed up as duties of abstention, of prevention, of acquiescence, of restoration and of reparation. Neutrals are expected to be impartial in their dealings with the belligerents; they must avoid preference or discrimination. Impartiality excludes such assistance to one of the belligerents as is detrimental to the other. They should give equal facilities to both the belligerents. The duties of impartiality comprises duty of abstention and duty of prevention.

1. Duties of Abstention

The duty of abstention is of a negative and passive character. A neutral state must not grant armed assistance or any other help to either side, such as, war ships and other war material. There should be no direct or indirect participation in the war in favour of either belligerent. However, private dealings are not prohibited. Private loans and trades are permitted. Neutral citizens even can cross the frontier and join one of the parties of the war as per Hague Convention of 1907.

2. Duties of Prevention

The duties of prevention are of a positive and active character. A neutral state should prevent recruitment, military operation or other warlike expedition. No corps combatents should be formed on its territory. It should disallow the establishment of belligerent prize courts and also the passage of landforces, barring wounded soldiers. Hence Belgium being neutral refused passage to German troops both in 1914 and 1940. But a neutral state is not obliged to prevent passage of belligerent war ships through its territorial waters, provided there is no indication that the territorial water was being used for naval operation. The limit of the right of a neutral state to permit the passage of belligerent men of war through its territorial waters was well illustrated by the case of Altmark.[2] The passage of belligerent war ships through straits may be allowed but here impartiality must be observed, as was decided in S.S. Wimbledon.[3] Further, neutral ports should not become asylum for belligerent prizes, or a refuge for belligerent ships. Since such ports are meant to serve international traffic on the sea, they may be used by the belligerent for limited purposes like repair and supply of fuel. Regarding the stay and repair of war ships the law of neutrality does not permit undue stay. They can stay in a neutral port for a maximun of 3 hours at a time. But on account of damage or stress of weather they can remain longer than 24 hours. However, it is to be noted that only civil repairs are allowed. As such repairs adding to the fighting capacity of the belligerent are disallowed. Neutrals should also prevent entry within its jurisdiction of military aircrafts and can compel them to alight if they entered in violation of air warfare rules of 1923. Lastly, they should not allow their territory to become information centres.

3. Duties of Acquiescence

Neutral states should not mind incidental damages during war operations, such as right of visit and search, and capture at sea. Unavoidably, the neutral state during war period is subject to certain restrictions.

4. Duties of Restoration

If a belligerent captures a prize in neutral waters, the neutral state owes a duty to restore the prize to the injured belligerent.

5. Duties of Reparation

"When a belligerent suffers loss through failure of a neutral state because of illwill or remissness to fulfil the obligation, a valid claim for satisfaction and redress arises."[4]

Case Law

In the Alabama Claims case[5] on reparation the fact of the case were as follows:

During the American Civil War (1861-65) a number of vessels, including Alabama, were built in English shipyard for the use of the Confederate Navy. Though unarmed when they left the English port they were presumably meant to be used against the American Commerce. Certainly they were supplied with arms at some neutral ports.

Alabama, which was built at Liverpool, had captured some 70 US vessels. Alabama was supplied with arms at Azores—a neutral territory, by 3 ships coming from England. On the US claim of compensation for the depradation by Alabama, Britain denied any responsibility. As per the Treaty of Washington (1871) both Britain and America agreed to constitute an arbitral tribunal. The tribunal found Britain liable for unneutral action and consequently Britain was asked to pay compensation amounting to 15,500,000 dollars to US. The Tribunal, however, disallowed the American claims for indirect damages. In this case it was held that a neutral government is bound to use due diligence to prevent the fitting out, arming or equipping within its jurisdiction of any vessel which it has reasonable ground to believe was intended for war purposes against a power with which it was at peace. Incidentally, Article 8 of the Hague Convention-XIII was based on this ruling.

The other leading cases on the subject are Altamark, Appam, Zamora, etc., which are discussed elswhere along with leading cases.

REFERENCES

1. LAWRENCE, in M.P. Tandon, *Public International Law*, op. cit., pp. 566-69.
2. MAHAJAN, V.D., *Public International Law*, op. cit., p. 673.
3. P.C.I.J. (1923), Series A No. 1.
4. LAWRENCE, *Principles of International Law* (ed), New York, P.H. Winfield op. cit., p. 654.
5. GREEN, C.L. op. cit., p. 23.

Chapter 23

Blockade

The institution of blockade dates back from 1584 and 1630 when the Dutch Government declared all the ports of Flanders in the power of Spain, to be blockaded. But it was not until the middle of the 19th century that the rules of international law relating to blockade became settled. The Declaration of Paris (1856) and the London Declaration (1909) have made valuable contribution to the development of blockade rules.

According to Oppenheim's definition "blockade is the blocking, by men of war, of the approach to the enemy coast, or a part of it for the purpose of preventing ingress or egress of vessels or aircrafts of all nations."[1] In other words, it is the interception by a belligerent of access to a place which is in the possession of his enemy.[2] But blockade is differnt from siege. Whereas siege aims at the capture of the besieged place, blockade only intercepts all intercourse by sea.

Characteristics of Modern Blockade

1. Blockade must be done by men of war though it may be reinforced by other means.
2. Only enemy coast or a part of it is to be the object of blockade.
3. It should check both the ingress or egress of ships.
4. Blockade to be admissible must be impartially applied to vessels and aircrafts of all nations.
5. It is a war-like operation. It is an act of war and effectively denies freedom of passage. Although it is a means of warfare against the enemy yet it equally concerns neutrals.

Forms of Blockade

(*i*) **Strategic/hostile blockade.** A blockade is termed strategic or hostile if it forms part of other military operations directed against the coast which is blockaded.

(*ii*) **Commercial/pacific blockade.** A blockade is commercial or pacific when it is declared with the object of diminishing the resources of enemy by cutting off its external intercourse and no military operation take place on the shore.

Essentials of Blockade

In order that a blockade may be binding and real, it must possess the following essential features:

(*a*) **Effectiveness.** The necessity of an effective blockade was realised during the first half of the 19th century. It is different from paper blockade which is not maintained by a sufficient force. The Declaration of Paris (1856) laid down that an effective blockade is one which is maintained by a force sufficient to prevent access to the enemy coast. However, it failed to define "sufficient force". Lord Chief Justice Cockburn observed in the case of Geipel *vs.* Smith: "In the eyes of law a blockade is effective if the enemy's ships are in such numbers and position as to render running the blockade a matter of danger, although some vessels may succeed ingetting through."[3] The London Declaration (1909) declared that "the question whether a blockade is effective is a question of fact."

(*b*) **Proper establishment.** It is required that it must be established by a competent authority. As per London Declaration, a declaration of blockade is made by the blockading power or by the naval authorities acting in its name, i.e., by the government or the Commander of navy.

(*c*) **Notification**. For an effective blockade, it is essential that it should be notified. The notification must specify the date when the blockade commences, the geographical limits of the coast line to which access is barred, and the period within which neutral vessels may come out. The notice of blockade must correspond to actual facts. Actual knowledge of blockade renders the vessel liable to confiscation. The Anglo-American practice recognises both the actual as well as constructive knowledge of blockade. But to the French practice the neutral vessel is unaffected by presumptions as to the continuance or cessation of a blockade. The Commander of the vessel is entitled to the individual warning from the blockading squadrons. Hence, a neutral vessel can make a first test of effectiveness of a blockade with impunity.

(*d*) **Impartiality**. Blockade is admissible only when there is a universal blockade. Any favour shown to a vessel renders it inoperative. It should be enforced impartially. In the case of "Franciska" British blockade of Riga during the Crimean War (1854-56) was held invalid by the Privy Council as there was relaxation to belligrent merchant vessels to the exclusion of neutrals.

(*e*) **Continuous maintetence.** When the blockading squadron is driven off by the hostile forces, the blockade becomes null and void. But it does not become invalid only because there is a temporary absence of the squadron on account of the stress of bad weather. However, when such weather is over original position must be resumed.

(*f*) **Exemption of neutral ports.** The blockading force must not bar access to neutral ports. They must be kept open for the ships.

(*g*) **Restriction on the area.** The geographical area specified in the notification must be strictly adhered to and the blockade should not be extended beyond it.

Long Distance Blockade

Long distance blockade was adopted during the First World War as a new strategy of maritime warfare. British Navy enforced a "long distance" blockade of Germany through ships and squadrons operating at times more than a thousand miles from German ports. It was done as a reprisal for submarine attacks without any regard to safety of passengers. This blockade was promptly challenged by neutrals, particularly the USA. The American contention was that "the British blockade was a blockade neither in law nor in practice nor in effect. But Britain justified the action on the ground of changed conditions of modern warfare which required that an effective blockade must be able to cover commerce with the enemy passing through neutral ports.

The "long distance" blockade was again resorted to during the Second World War by Britain and France on the plea of total economic warfare against the enemy. But this did not prove to be of much use on account of open front on the East. Britain sought to simplify her blockade by issuing orders-in-council in 1915 and 1942 which introduced a system of navicerts. It laid down that the goods might become liable to seizure in the absence of navicerts to cover them. There was an assumption that unnavicerted goods had an enemy destination. These measures were repeatedly used in wars in the form of reprisals on the principle that a belligerent who possesses the affective command of the sea is entitled to deprive his opponent of the use thereof for the purpose of navigation.

It is thus clear that the old system under which the blockading squadrons remained constantly close a blockaded port proves no longer feasible in the modern conditions of warfare, especially due to the extended range of shore batteries, torpedo boats, and the action of submarines, which necessitate the blockading force to remain out of sight of the blockaded coast. Further, the blockading naval squadron is also exposed to serious attacks by the enemy from the air. Hence Higgins and Colombos observe: "in the present circumstances the institution of an actual blockade by a cordon of stationary ships is impracticable." The establishment of 'close blockade' having become impossible, the legality of long range blockade cannot be challenged if the right of a belligerent to cut off the seaborne commerce of his enemy is recognised. They are valid provided they effectively prevent the ingress or egress of all vessels and goods from the blockaded area by sea, and provided also they are properly announced and maintained.

Commencement of Blockade

A blockade does not come into being ipso facto by the outbreak of war. Notification has always been essential for the establishment of a blockade, although the Anglo-American practice consider knowledge on the part of a neutral vessel of an existing blockade sufficient to justfy her condemnation for breach of blockade. They maintain a distinction between a so-called de facto blockade and a notified blockade. The moment a blockade is instituted, it becomes valid as regards ingress, but in the case of egress, the blockading Commander is under an obligation to grant a certain length of time within which netural vessels might leave the blockaded ports unhindered.

Cessation of Blockade

A blockade can come to an end in the following ways:

(*a*) On the termination of war; (*b*) if it is withdrawn by the blockading power by notificaton; (*c*) if it ceases to be effective; (*d*) if the blockaded port is captured by the blockading authorities; and (*e*) when the blockading squadron is driven off or defeated by a hostile force.

Breach of Blockade

An unpermitted ingress or egress of a vessel in spite of blockade is called a breach of blockade. According to Sir Willian Scott, to constitute a violation of blockade three things must be proved: (*a*) the existence of an actual blockade; (*b*) the party violating the blockade knew the fact of the existence of it; and (*c*) some act of violation.[4]

The practice of states as to what constitutes a breach has varied. The French practice sought to restrict an attempt so break blockade to the employment of force by a vessel for the purpose of passing through. To Japan, a breach takes place when a vessel endeavoured to pass the line of blockade with or without force. But the Anglo-American practice went beyond this. Applying the doctrine of continuous voyage, they hold that an attempt to break blockade was committed by a vessel, which although destined for a neutral or an unblockaded port, in reality intended, after touching there, to go on to a blockaded port. A great variation also exists regarding prior notification. England and USA share the view that it is enough to establish presumptively that those incharge of the neutral vessel knew that a blockade had been established. But Italy and France demand that the Commander of a neutral vessel is entitled to get a warning by the blockading squadron on approaching the blockaded area. It is, however, settled that in case of blockade by notification, notice is presumed if it has been duly issued and sufficient time has elapsed since then to enable the neutral government to receive the same.

Penalty for Breach of Blockade

After capture the vessel running the blockade is sent to a port for adjudication by a prize court. The mere intention to break it is not condemnable. It must be coupled with some act showing an attempt to enter the port, as was held in the Zamora case. The ship and cargo both are captured when there is breach of blockade. The owners of the cargo are deemed to have known about it when the shipment was made unless they prove ignorance of the blockade. After the decision of the Court the crew can be released. There is confiscation of both the cargo and the vessel if both belong to the same owner. But if ownership differs the cargo is confiscated only in case of contraband of war or if the owners knew of the blockade at the time of shipment.

Case Law

In the case of Springbok only the cargo was confiscated, as the owners of the vessel were ignorant of the ultimate destination.

In the case of Franciska[5] (a Danish vessel) the plea of ignorance was held invalid as the captain of the ship was aware of the blockade. However, its capture was rendered invalid because of relaxation granted to belligerent merchant vessels.

In the case of Zamora[6] it was observed that mere intention to violate a blockade does not render a ship liable to capture or condemnation. In this case it was also observed by Lord Parker that an order declaring a blockade though prima facie justifies the capture of vessels entering the blockaded port but at the same time it does not preclude evidence to show that it was ineffective and therefore unlawful.

REFERENCES

1. Oppenheim, *International Law*, op. cit., Vol. II, p. 768.
2. Hall in M.P. Tandon, *Public International Law*, op. cit., p. 574,
3. (1872), L.R. 7 Q.B. p. 410.
4. The Betsey, I.C. Rob, p. 92.
5. 10 MOO, P.C, p. 36.
6. (1916) 2 A.C. p. 77.

Chapter 24

Prize Law and Prize Courts

Any property of the enemy captured on the high seas during war is known as prize. A title to such property follows Prize Courts' determination. All civilised belligerents establish Prize Courts for the protection of neutral property and the proper adjustment of the claims of captors.

Osborn defines Prize Courts as "courts specially constituted for the purpose of deciding question of meritime capture in times of war according to international law." According to Lawrence, "they are municipal tribunal set up by belligerents for the purpose of deciding upon the validity of the captures."[1]

Functions of a Prize Court

According to Pitt Cobbet, its functions are as follows:

1. To enquire into cases of maritime capture.
2. To decree condemnation where the property proves to be lawful prize.
3. To award restitution where it is not with just compensation.
4. Incidentally, to protect the interest of all against rapine and disorder.[2]

Jurisdictions of a Prize Court

The jurisdiction of a Prize Court extends to captures made on high seas, on land by naval forces, and to ransom and connected questions of damages. The decisions of the Prize Court is conclusive. It can't be reviewed by other country. The force of res judicata of decisions is also recognised. Finally, ad judicated issues cannot be reopened except by way of appeal.

Each State has to organise its own courts to regulate the procedure. Nevertheless, the procedures to be adopted have certain international aspects. Both the parties of the disputes, are to get hearing and the decision is to be based on international law. The burden of proof lies on the captors, as against the procedure obtaining in civil and criminal courts. However, it is to be noted that prize court cannot be established in a neutral country. They are to be established either in the territory of the belligerent or in the territory of an ally or in occupied territory.

The Status of Prize Courts

Prize Courts have international character. They are open to all irrespective of nationality. According to Lawrence, "they are Municipal Courts to administer International Law." As such they are responsible to their own state. Although international law is said to be their source but when legislation contrary to international law is thrust on them, judges cannot help. Such conflict, however, arises rarely. The decisions of these courts are respected in proportion to their impartiality. In the opinion of Oppenheim, "a prize court is a national court constituted by municipal law." Every state is to enact only such statutes that conform with international law. But at the same time British courts are bound to apply an Act of Parliament. Trials of captured neutral vessels constitute municipal matters. Neutral states, therefore, are not represented. "The Court is, therefore, international in function but national in constitution and organisation," as Oppenheim has aptly observed. To quote Pitt Cobbet, "Prize Courts are national tribunals but created for enforcing international law."

Case Laws

In the case of Fox, Stowell observed: "the two propositions that the court is bound to administer international law and to enforce King's Orders-in-Council are not inconsistent as the orders are to conform to the principles of international law."[3]

In the case of Zamora,[4] Lord Parker held that the Prize Court was bound by Act of Parliament but not Orders-in-Council inconsistent with rules of international law. But he added that the Prize Court would not ignore executive orders which mitigated the rights of the Crown in favour of a neutral or enemy and was to give effect to them.

Destruction of Prize

When captured ships and cargoes are enemy property and cannot be brought to the shore they can be destroyed. The doctrine of necessity justifies such destruction. However, it does not apply to neutral property. Neutrals can claim indemnity in case of destruction. The London Declaration (1909), however, provided that even neutral spips can be destroyed if they carry contraband. But in case of destruction the captor must remove crew, ships, paper and cargo and send them to a port of adjudication for satisfying the Prize Courts that it was lawful.

International Prize Court

It is strongly suggested that there should be an International Prize Court in order to meet the ends of justice. Since Prize Courts are national courts, there is bound to be uncouscious bias in the minds of Judges. During stress of war impartiality is difficult to achieve. Taking into consideration all these handicaps, Germany and Britain at one time advocated for an International Prize Court. But since there was no codified system of precise prize law, the proposal fell through. Any way, it is more feasible to allow the existing International Court of Justice to hear apeals from the Prize Courts.

REFERENCES

1. LAWRENCE, *Principles of International Law*, op. cit., p. 460.
2. COBBET, PITT, *Leading Cases on International Law*, Vol. II, 5th Ed. p. 258.
3. THE FOX AND OTHERS, Edwards, *Adm. Report*, p. 312.
4. [(1916) 2 A.C.77]

Chapter 25

Law of Contraband of War

The term "contraband" is derived from two Latin words contra and bondum meaning in defence of injunction. But in ordinary usage it means prohibited goods. In international law a definite technical meaning is given to the term contraband. It is used for goods which are considered objectionable and liable to be captured and condemned. According to Oppenheim, "contraband of war is the designation of such goods as are forbidden by either belligerent to be carried to the enemy on the ground that they enable it to carry on the war with greater vigour."[1] It denotes such articles as are considered objectionable to be carried by a neutral to a belligerent because they are calculated to be of direct service in carrying war or otherwise assist one of the belligerents in the conduct of war. The object of the law of contraband is to cripple the enemy's commerce. In the words of Pitt Cobbet, "the basis of the law of contraband is the right of a belligerent to condemn neutral property which is destined for the military use of his enemy."[2]

Division of Contraband Commodities

The unratified Declaration of London (1909) divided all commodities into three classes on the pattern of Grotian Classification: (1) *Absolute contraband*—It includes all military articles, warships, projectiles, etc. These things carry the guilt on their face. Such goods are to be condemned whether the carriage of goods is direct or entails trans-shipment or subsequent transportation by land. (2) *Conditional contraband*—It includes articles which are used both in war and peace. This class of commodity comprises foodstuffs, coal, forage, grain, fabric, gold and silver in coin or bullion, vehicles, boats, fuel, railway material, etc. Such articles are liable to capture if distined for the armed forces of a belligerent or found on board a vessel bound for a territory of enemy and when they were not to be discharged in an intervening neutral port. In 1917, the British Government issued a list including 34 kinds of articles under the heading of conditional contraband and during the Second World War all kinds of foodstuffs, forage, clothing were included in the British list of conditional contraband. Germany followed her example in both the World Wars. (3) *Non-contraband*—This category includes things that are useless for warlike purposes such as raw cotton, wool, silk, oil seeds, rubber, clocks, watches, etc. They are not treated as contraband in any circumstances.

For absolute contraband any kind of enemy destination is all that is required (Article 30 of London Declaration), conditional contraband are liable to capture if destined either for armed forces or government department of enemy state. There is a presumption of enemy destination if they are consigned to a fortified place of enemy, to one of his bases of operation or to an enemy contractor of the government. Lawrance maintains that the use to which the goods are to be put fixes their guilt or innocence, the destination is proof of use, and the papers are proof of destination.

Penalty for Carrying Contraband

Articles 39 and 40 of London Declaration provide for the confiscation of enemy vessels if the contraband constitutes more than half of the cargo. In case the goods are condemned and vessels released, she may be made liable to pay cost of proceeding. If the Prize Court decides the cargo to be a good prize then it is confiscated. However, in exceptional cases the vessels are liable to confiscation, e.g., if ships belong to the owner to the eargo, or more than half of the cargo is contraband, or if false destination or false payers are shown.

Relationship between Contraband and Blockade

The two essential elements of the concept of contraband are the character of goods and an enemy destination. In the case of blockade all merchant ships of whatever nationality are confiscated irrespective of the nature of the cargo. "The object of blockade is not only to stop the importation of supplies but to prevent export as well."[3] The law of blockade is limited in area, while the law of contraband is limited in scope. In contraband it is the cargo which is the main object of capture but in blockade the ship or vessel is the target. However, the two world wars have obliterated all distinction between contraband and blockade. Now the law of contraband is adopted to perform the function of blockade and without the narrow geographical limitation to which the old blockade were restricted. In this connection Smith observes: "now the whole of the sea borne trade can be destroyed to jeopardise the interest of the enemy under whatever flag and through whatever countries it may pass."[4] For technical reasons, blockade in old sense has now become impossible under the condition of modern warfare. "From lawyers point of view as a result of two wars the law of contraband has been merged with that of blockade."

Doctrine of Continuous Voyage

The doctrine of continuous voyage dates back from the time of the Anglo-French Wars at the end of the eighteeth century and is connected with the application of the Rule of 1756. According to Pitt Cobbet, "the doctrine of continuous voyage consists in treating an adventure, which involves the carriage of goods in the first instance to a neutral port and thence to some ulterior end hostile destination, as being for certain purposes only one transportion, with all the consequences which would attach if the neutral port had not interposed.[5]" The doctrine was occasioned by the fact that some neutral vessels sought to evade capture of contraband goods by breaking their voygage into two parts, first going to a neutral port (according to papers) and then reloading and trying to reach their real destination, i.e., the belligerent port. Similar tricks were used to break blockade as well. The application of the doctrine could foil their attempt to evade the rule of contraband and blockade. For its application, however, the interposition of an immediate port is necessary and transportation is to be devided into two parts. The vessel can be seized on the very first part of the voyage, and condemned upon proof of intention of the owner to continue the voyage.

As regards its application to blockade, it permitted the cargo to be captured at any stage of voyage, if the same destined to be carried through blokade. Article 39 of the London Declaration made contraband liable to capture, it being immaterial whether the carriage of goods was direct or entailed transshipment or even a subsequent transport by land.

Leading Cases

In 'Maria',[6] Lord Stowell while explaining the doctrine observed: it is a settled principle that the mere touching any port without importing the cargo into the common stock of the country will not alter the nature of the voyage which must be considered as a voyage to the country to which the vessel is actually going for the purpose of delivering the cargo at the ultimate port.

In 'Bermuda',[7] the court observed: "A transportation from one point to another remains continuous so long as intent remains unchanged, no matter what stoppages or transshipment intervene."

In 'Peterhoff',[8] the doctrine was carried to the farthest extent when the alleged ulterior destination of the contraband cargo was applied to land transport as well. The US applied the doctrine even if the ship was changed during the course of voyage. She also applied it to breach of blockade, if the intention was to send cargo to blockaded port by the same ship or another one or by land transport.

In 'Kim'[9] Sir Samuel Evans observed: "the contraband articles are said to be of an infectious nature and they contaminate the whole cargo belonging to the same owner. The innocence of any particular article is not usually admitted to exempt it from the general confiscation."

In the 'Springbok'[10], the US Supreme Court condemned the cargo of a British vessel captured enroute to Nassau, because the character of the cargo left no room for doubt that its true destination was a blockaded port.

RIGHT OF ANGARY

The word angary is derivied from Persian language. The right of angary is a very old right. It was in practice not only in the Middle Ages but also in ancient times. However, this right fell into disuse during the 18th and 19th centuries. But is was revived in the present century in a modified form.

According to Oppenheim, "it is a right of belligerents to destroy or use, in case of necessity, for the purpose of offence and defence, neutral property on their territory or on enemy territoy or on the open Sea."[11] In other words, it denotes the right of a belligerent in times of war or other public danger to use or to destroy neutral property. It affords a belligerent to requisition vessels, rolling stock, aircraft, etc., belonging to a neutral. The principle behind this right is that the supreme interest of the state overrides all laws. To quote Pollock, "it is the right of a state to requisition foreign ships, aircrafts and other means of transportation which are urgently required for the purpose of transportation which are at the time of requisition within its territorial jurisdiction, but such requisition can be made in time of national emergency subject to payment of full compensation, while the services of foreign personnel (crew) can't be compelled in any circumstances."

Features of Jus Angariae

(1) Requisition of property under this right can only be made during national emergency.

(2) The belligerent exercising this right must pay full compensation to the neutral concerned.

(3) The services of foreign crew of the ships or aircrafts cannot be requisitioned.

(4) The right cannot be exercised by a belligerent in a territory under military occupation.

(5) The right cannot be exercised beyond the regions of war.

(6) The neutrals themselves may also exercise this right during grave national emergency. Thus the right of angary is a sovereign right of every state.

ARTICLE 19 OF CONVENTION-V OF THE SECOND HAGUE

Conference specially recognises the right of engary in allowing a belligerent to utilise, in case of absolute necessity, property belonging to neutrals subject to payment of compensation.

The right of angary however is not absolute. It can be exercised under the following limitations:

(*a*) The right can be exercised only by a sovereign state and the requisitioned goods and means of transport or any other property must be within the territorial jurisdiction of the state requisitioning them.

(*b*) The right does not extend beyond the teritorrial limits of the requisitioning state.

(*c*) The right does not extend to a territory under military occupation.

(*d*) The right is to be exercised only under emergency situations and the property utilised must be paid for.

(*e*) The services of the foreign crew of the ships or aircrafts are immune from this right.

(*f*) The neutral property simply passing through the belligerent state is also immune to capture in the exercise of this right.

(*g*) This right would not be used to justify the destruction of property of the neutral as destinguished from appropriation.

During the First World War, the right was practised on a very large scale, particularly by Britiain, USA, France, Italy who requisitioned a number of Dutch (neutral) vessels. Similarly, during the Second World War the USA (a neutral state) passed an Act in June 1941 under which she declared that she would purchase or requisition any foreign ship remaining within her territorial waters subject to the payment of compensation. This is the most prominent example of the exercise of this right by a neutral state in recent times.

In the case of Zamora,[12] Lord Parker observed that a belligerent has, in proper case, the power to requisition ships and goods of neutrals in the custody of the Prize Courts for adjudication. He, however, added that the right can be exercised only in certain circumstances and for certain purposes. He held that the requisition could be allowed if (*a*) goods were urgently required for defence; (*b*) when a real question was to be tried; (*c*) when the Prize Court determines judicially whether the right is exercisable.

Some writers question the very right of angary. They argue that it is an act of self-defence, pure and simple and based on the doctrine of military necessity and hence already covered under the right of self-preservation.

REFERENCES

1. OPPENHEIM, *International Law*, op. cit. Vol. II. p. 799.
2. COBBET, PITT, in M.P. Tondon, *Public International Law*, op. cit, p. 581.
3. HIGGINS AND COLMBOS, *International Law of the Sea*, 2nd Ed., p. 539.
4. SMITE, H.A., *The Crisis in the Law of Nations*, p. 59.
5. COBBET, PITT in M.P. Tandon, *Public International Law*, op. cit. p. 585.
6. (1799) 5 C. Rob. 3.
7. 3 Wallace, 1.
8. (1866) 5 Wallace, 56.
9. (1915) Probate Division, p. 215.
10. (1856) 5 Wallace, 1.
11. OPPENHEIM, *Internationnl Law*, Vol. ÍI, 7th Ed., pp. 761, 765.
12. (1916) 2,A.C. 77.

Chapter 26

Leading Cases on International Law

1. CHUNG CHI CHEUNG *VS.* THE KING (1939) [(1939) A.C. 160 AND AIR 1939 P.C. 69] (TERRITORIAL JURISDICTION AND IMMUNITIES)

The appellant (Chung Chi Cheung) was a cabin boy on board a Chinese armed public ship. While the vessel was in Hong Kong territorial waters, he killed its Captain and wounded himself also. Both the murdered man and the appellant were British nationals in Chinese service. Extradition proceedings instituted by Chinese authorities had failed and Cheung was convicted and sentenced to death by the Hong Kong Court. The cabin boy then appealed to the Privy Council.

The question before the Judicial Committee of the Privy Council was whether the local British Court (Hong Kong) had jurisdiction to try the appellant for crimes committed on board a public ships of other nation while in British territorial waters.

The Judicial Committee held that there was no valid ground to oppose jurisdiction of the Hong Kong High Court. Since the request for extradiction had failed, the Chinese Government could be taken to have consented to the British Court in Hong Kong exercising jurisdiction and hence the British Court was competent to try the case.

Admitting that immunities extend to Sovereign, his envoy, his property, his armed public vessel, the Judicial Committee took the view that a public ship in foreign waters is not to be treated as territory of its own nation or as 'floating island'. The Chinese Government could equally exercise jurisdiction in this case, if her request for extradition had not failed.

In deciding the appeal, Lord Akkin observed: "the principles of international law are incorporated with Municipal Law if they are not inconsistent with Statutory Law. International law therefore had no validity save in so far as its principles are adopted by our domestic law."

2. PAQUETE HABANA AND LOLA *VS.* UNITED STATES (1899)
[(1899) 175 U.S. 677]
(USAGES AND CUSTOMS OF INTERNATIONAL LAW)

The Paquete Habana and Lola (Spanish fishing boats) were captured by the US warships which were engaged at that time in the blockade of the north coast of Cuba. None of them carried military supplies or had a knowledge of the blockade. The Prize Court had upheld the capture of these boats. But the Supreme Court on appeal reversed the order of the lower court holding that the fishing boats were exempt from capture. In deciding this appeal Justice Gray observed: "In the absence of treaty or any controlling executive act or judicial decisions resort must be had to the customs and usages and as evidence of these to works of jurists and commentators. He added that fishing vessels and unarmed crew should be free from capture as Prize of War.

3. THE PARLEMENT BELGE (1880)
[(1880) 5 P.D. 197]
(TERRITORIAL JURISDICTION: IMMUNITIES AND LIMITATIONS)

A Belgian mail packet, which was also used for trading purposes, collided against Daring, a Britishship, in the Dover Harbour. The first proceedings in this case of collision took place in the Admiralty Division. Later on, the Court of Appeal observed that "a publicly owned vessel was exempt from a suit in rem for damages. The court held that even though an action in rem was an action against the property only, a suit could not be brought. It maintained that it would not exercise jurisdiction over the person or public property of a foreign sovereign and that it could not even inquire into the declaration of a foreign sovereign as to the nature of the ship.

4. MIGHELL *VS.* SULTAN OF JAHORE (1894)
[(1894) I.Q.B. 149]
(TERRITORIAL JURISDICTION: IMMUNITIES AND LIMITATIONS)

The Sultan of Jahore (an independent kingdom in Malay Peninsula) while in England assumed the name of Albert Barker in order to make love with Mighell as an English man. The Sultan had even promised to marry Mighell at one stage. But when he refused to marry ultimately, a charge of breach of promise was lodged against the Sultan by Mighell. The Court of Appeal in this case held that it had no jurisdiction over the Sultan as he was a Sovereign, unless he himself submitted to it. Lord Esher who decided the case quoted the Parlēment Belge case by way of precedent to support his decision.

5. ARANTZAZU MENDI *VS*. REPUBLIC OF SPAIN [(1939) P. 37: 2 B.I.L.C. 188] (RECOGNITION AND TERRITORIAL JURISDICTION)

Arantzazu Mendi was an English ship registered at Bilbao port, which was taken into possession by the forces of General Franco during the Spanish Civil War in 1937. When the ship arrived in London in August 1937, her owners issued a writ in rem for possession and the ship was taken possession of by the Admiralty Marshall of Britain. The Republican Government of Spain, there upon, entered a conditional appearance to the writ. In 1938, Franco issued a decree requisitioning it. The Republican Government also issued a similar decree on the same day.

The question that fell for consideration was to whom the ship legally belonged—the de jure or the de facto Government. The British Foreign Office reply to the first court was that it recognised the Nationalist Government of Franco as de facto Government and hence the Court set aside the writ of the Republican Government and the warrent of arrest. The decision of the Court of Appeal upholding this finding was affirmed by Lord Atkin in the House of Lord as well.

6. WEST RAND CENTRAL GOLD MINING CO. LTD *VS*. THE KING (1905) [(1905) 2. K.B. 391] (STATE SUCCESSION)

The West Rand Central Gold Mining Company was an English firm working a gold mine in Transval. Two parcels of gold belonging to the company were seized by the officials of the former Republican Government of Transval. As a sequal to Boer War, the South African Republic was conquered by Britain in 1899 and the latter ultimately annexed the territory. The company, therefore, sought to recover the gold packets from the successor, the British Government.

Lord Alverston, Chief Justice of the King's Bench Division, pronounced that upon principle the proposition that by international law the Conqueror, was bound to fulfil such obligation could not be sustained. He laid down: "Whatever had received the common consent of civilized nations must have received the assent of our country." He added that any doctrine so invoked must be one really accepted as binding and international law sought to be applied must be proved by satisfactory evidence The claims of Company to recover from the Successor Government the gold or value thereof was therefore disallowed, on the basis of customary international law. But the modern view on the contrary favours recognition of continuation of concession allowed by the preceeding state. The modern practice therefore had modified the doctrine of non-succession as was laid down in this case. The Permanent Court of International Justice in its advisory opinion in 'German Settlers in Poland' case (1923) too had supported the modern view. The Court maintained: "a cession of territory does not operate as a cession of the property belonging to its inhabitants. The same view was held in Mavrommatis-Palestine Concession Case (1924) when R.C.I.J. maintained that the British Government as mandatory power could not rescind the Concession allowed to this Greak Subject (Mavrommatis) by the proceeding Turkish Government, though no indemnity was allowed to him as his additional claim.

7. S.S. LOTUS
[(1927) SERIES A. NO. 10]
(TERRITORIAL JURISDICTION AND COLLISION)

On August 2, 1926, a French Steam ship, the S.S. Lotus, proceeding to Constantinople collided with a Turkish Collier, Boz Kourt, on the open sea 6 miles off Cape Sigov. The result was that the Boz Kourt sank and 8 Turkish lost their lives.

As soon as the Lotus arrived at Constantinople on August 3, the Turkish authorities requested Lt. Demons to give evidence, regarding collision. On August 5, both the Captains on Lotus were put under arrest without giving any previous notice to the French Consul General.

At the Criminal Court Lt. Demons submitted that the Turkish Court had no jurisdiction to try him. But this plea was overruled, and Lt. Demons was sentenced to 8 days' imprisonment and a fine of £ 22. The other Captain (Hassan Bay) received a slightly heavier sentence.

The French Government demanded release and transfer of the case. Ultimately, by an agreement between them (1926) the matter was referred to the Hague Court.

Two questions fell for consideration before the World Court: (1) Whether Turkey had acted against international law in pursuance of Turkish law, in the trial of the Lotus Captain; (2) If the reply was in the affirmative, what pecuniary remuneration was due to Captains.

The World Court answered the first question in the negative but significantly, in order to get the majority verdict the president of the Court had to exercise his casting vote. The plea of Turkey was that Article 15 of the Lausanne Convention allowed her jurisdiction in the case, if the latter's (Italian) law did not conflict with international law principle. Further, jurisdiction is essentially territorial; it cannot be exercised by a state outside its territory except by virtue of permissive rule derived from custom or Convention.

The French Government on the other hand advanced three arguments:

(1) The offence took place on the French Vessel (the Lotus).

(2) Exclusive jurisdiction belongs to the State whose flag a ship is flying.

(3) This principle is specially applicable in collision case.

The World Court challenged and overruled all these arguments. It held that the offence was an act of negligence and imprudence having its origin on board the Lotus while its effects made themselves felt on board the Boz Kourt, i.e., on a place forming a part of Turkish territory. These two elements are inseparable. It is, therefore, a case of concurrent jurisdiction.

The majority of the judges rejected the pleas of the French Government but 6 Judges gave dissenting opinion and only the casting vote helped the majority view.

But now the French view is taken to be sounder one, because public vessels now enjoy immunity on the high seas. This is particularly so in times of peace. Here in this case the collision took place when there was no war. Both the Brussels Convention (1952) and the International Law Commission support the French view. The French view was adopted by the Geneva Convention of 1958 on the Sea Law. Hence the doctrine of 'objective jurisdiction' which assumes that the place where the effect of an act is produced is the place where it was actually committed has been rejected. In other words, in case of collission on the high seas of only the flag state causing such collision has jurisdiction, and as such the theory of concurrent jurisdiction is superseded.

8. CORFU CHANNEL CASE (1946)
[I.C.J. REPORTS 1940, P. 4]
(MARITIME BELT, TERRITORIAL JURISDICTION AND TORTS)

The north Corfu Channel constitutes a frontier between Albania and Greece, a part of which lies wholly within the territorial waters of these states. The Channel was swept by the British Navy in October 1944 when there were no mines and the route was found safe. On May 15, 1946, the British Cruisers (Orion and Superb) while passing southward through the Channel were fired, by the Albanian battery. Again, on October 22, 1946, two British Warships were damaged by striking mines in Albanian territorial waters. The explosion resulted in loss of life also. Subsequently, on November 12 and 13, the British Navy Swept the Channel without seeking Albanian authority and discovered a newly laid field of anchored mines at the place of explosion. Albania vehemetly protested against this mine sweeping operation, and referred the matter to the Security Council. Ultimately, by a special agreement between the two countries the World Court took up the case.

Two questions arose for decision before the International Court of Justice: (1) Is Albania responsible for the explosion on October 22, 1946? (2) Has the UK violated the sovereignty of Albania because of the mine swpeeping operation? The Court held Albania responsible for the explosion. It recognised Albanian failure to carry out its duties after the explosion and, therefore, decided that she should pay compensation amounting to £ 8,43,947 to UK (by 11 to 5 votes). The Court added that since the channel belongs to the class of International waterways, even war ships can go through it in times of peace. The second question related to mine Sweeping operation by the Royal Navy on November 12 and 13, 1946. On this question the Court rejected out of hand the British Plea of self-defence. It regarded the alleged right of intervention as the manifestation of a policy of force. It maintained that the operation was indeed a violation of Albania's Sovereignty.

9. HAYA DE LA TORRE
[I.C.J. REPORTS (1951), P. 71]
(EXTRADITION AND ASYLUM)

Haya de La Torre, a peruvian national and a political leader, accused in having instigated a military rebellion, was granted asylum in the Columbian Embassy at Lima. On the matter being referred to the International Court of Justice the Court observed that although the Havana Convention (1928) expressly prescribed the surrender of common criminals to the local authorities, no obligation of this kind existed in respect to political offenders. It, however, reiterated its earlier view that asylum had been irregularly granted and that although on this ground Peru was entitled to demand its termination,

Columbia was not bound to surrender the refugee.

10. ANGLO-NORWEGIAN FISHERIES CASE (1951)
[I.C.J. REPORTS 1951, P. 116]
(LIMITS OF TERRITORIAL WATERS)

A Royal decree defining Precisely the extent of the zone reserved for Norwegian Fishermen on that part of the coast which extended from the Finnish frontiers to a point on the Southern side of the opening of the Vestfjord was promulgated on the 12th July 1935. The Government of the UK applied to the International Court of Justice on 28th September 1949 for declaring the principles of International law which would be applied in defining base lines and by reference to which the Government of Norway was entitled to delimit a fisheries zone so as to reserve it exclusively for its own nationals.

The Court held that the method employed for the delimination of the fisheries zone by the Royal Norwegian decree of July 1935, was not contrary to International Law and that the base line fixed by the said decree in application of this method was not contrary to international principle. The Court further held that Norway like other states was entitled to determine not only the breadth of the territorial sea but also the manner in which it was to be reckoned in accordance with the general principles of the existing international law. The World Court allowed four miles a territorial water limit drawn from not low water mark, as Norway's coast was not uniform.

11. ICELAND FISHERIES JURISDICTION CASE (1974)
[I.C.J. REPORTS 1974]
(EXCLUSIVE ECONOMIC ZONE & FISHERIES)

Iceland is a barren island on the North Atlantic ocean near the Arctic circle. Ever since its independence from Denmark (1944) it has been concerned about its fisheries, which is the mainstay of her economy in its continuing struggle to protect from foreign depradation its precious fisheries resources providing vital food supply for its people and 90% of its export earnings. Iceland in a desperate attempts to ward off British travelers fishing in its coastal waters sought to extend its fishery limits to 200 nautical miles. Since she was no match in this 'Cod war' to the Navy of Britain that once used to boast of ruling the wave, she referred the matter to the World Court. In its judgement on 25 July 1974 the World Court refused to pronounce on the direct assertion of the UK that

Iceland's unilateral extension of its exclusive fisheries jurisdiction is without foundation in international law and is invalid. On the basis of British historical and special interest in the disputed waters the Court declared that Iceland's extension of exclusive fisheries zones was not opposable to the UK and could not be enforced against it though Iceland might claim preferential rights in these waters. Significantly, the Court abstained from ruling that such extension of fisheries zone limits beyond the territorial sea constitute a breach of international law.

12. ZAMORA (1916)
[(1916) 2 A.C. 77]
(PRIZE COURT, INTERNATIONAL LAW *VS.* MUNICIPAL LAW, NEUTRALITY, BLOCKADE, ANGARY)

The Zamora, a Swedish vessel, belonging to a neutral country, while carrying a Cargo of copper and grain from New York to Stock holm (Sweden) was stopped by a British Cruiser on April 8, 1915 and was taken to a British port. A writ was issued by the Procurator General on April 19, 1915 claiming confiscation of the Cargo as well as the ship (Zamora) on the ground that more than half of the Cargo (Copper) was contraband. A summon requisitioned the copper pending adjudication by the Prize Court under the Order of Prize Court Rule, 1914 after giving an undertaking for payment into the Court on behalf of Crown of the appraised value of the Cargo. The owner of Cargo filed objection against requisition. But the President of the Probate, Divorce and Admiralty Division, Sir Samuel Evans, ordered the requisition. Thereupon the owner of the Cargo preferred an appeal to the Privy Council. The Judicial Committee of the Privy Council reversed the decisions of the previous court.

The questions that fell for consideration before the Judicial Committee of the Privy Council were (1) whether an order of confiscation was binding on the Prize Court and (2) whether under Principle of international law the court has a right to requisition vessels or goods in the custody of the Prize Court pending the decision as to both condemnation or release.

It was contended by the British Government that the Prize Court rules derive their force from orders of King-in-Council and these rules are statutory and binding. The Judicial Committee held that the King-in-Council or any branch of the Executive had no power to prescribe or alter the law to be determined by court of law unless, of course, such orders mitigate the rigour of international law or the crown's rights in favour of the neutral or the enemy. The Prize

Court cannot act judicially if it is bound to take orders from one of the parties to the proceedings. Further, the prize court, though a municipal court, is bound to administer the law of nations and not municipal law. If an Order-in-Council were binding on the prize court, such court might be compelled to act contrary to the express terms of the commission from which it derives its jurisdiction. It cannot be disputed that a prize court is bound by the legislative enactments of our sovereign state. If the Act of Parilament is inconsistent with international law, the prize court in giving effect to the Act would no longer be administering international law. The fact that prize courts would be bound by an Act of Parliament affords no ground for arguing that they are bound by the Executive Order of the King-in-Council also. But these Orders-in-Council will be given due weight if found mitigating Crown rights in favour of the enemy or the neutral. The primary duty of the court is to preserve the res (property) for delivery to the persons who ultimately establish their title. The inherent power of the court as to sale or requisition is confined to cases when res is perishable or its preservation is difficult.

It was also observed that the court can allow requisition to belligerent only under three conditions:

(1) The vessels or goods in question must be urgently required for use in connection with the defence of the realm, the prosection of the war, or other matters involving national security.

(2) There must be a real question to be tried, so that it would be improper to order an immediate release.

(3) The right must be enforced by an application to the Prize Court, which must determine judicially whether under the particular circumstances of the case, the right is exerciseable.

Their Lordships concluded that the order appealed from was wrong, not because, as contended by the appellants that there is no right at all for the belligerent to requisition ships or goods in the custody of Prize Court, but because the Judge had before him no satisfactory evidence that such right as exercisable. Since it was not proved that the copper was urgently needed for national security purposes, the order for requisition of copper was unjustified, and hence authorized a claim for damages to the owner.

This monumental judgement of Lord Parker is the bedrock of the entire case law with regard to Prize Court, relation of international law to municipal law, the scope of Order-in-Council in relation to Act of Parliament, the right to requisition Cargo and Vessels, and blockade as well. Regarding blockade Lord Parker's ruling was that mere intention to violate a blockade does not render a ship liable to capture or condemnation. He maintained that an order determining a blockade though *prima facie* justified the capture of vessels entering the blockaded port but it does not preclude evidence to show that it was ineffective and therefore unlawful.

13. PETERHOFF (1866)
[5. WALLACE, 28]
(BLOCKADE CONTRABAND AND CONTINUOUS VOYAGE)

There was a shipment of Contraband goods from England to Matamoras, a neutral port on the Mexican side of the Rio Grande, during the American Civil War. It was alleged that the ship was intended to violate the blockade of the coasts of the Southern Confederacy though apparently destined for a neutral port. Incidentally, this port was of immense importance for trade.

The Prize Court of the US condemned both the Cargo and the vessel. But on appeal to the Supreme Court the decision was reversed, as Peterhoff had not violated the blockade, as contended by America. Yet the Court condemned that part of the cargo consisting of military articles whose evident destination was the Confederate States. The vessel and non-contraband cargo, however, were released. The Court further added that a blockage is not to be extended by construction. The Mexican side of Rio Grande was open to commerce of neutrals as the whole river was not under blockade. The trade of neutrals with belligerents in articles not contraband is absolutely free, unless interrupted by blockade. The articles of Contraband character destined in fact to a state in rebellion were liable to capture though primarily destined to Matamoras. Justice Chase observed: "We are obliged to conclude that the portion of the Cargo which we have characterised as contraband must be condemned."

The significance of Peterhoff lies in the fact that the doctrine of continuous voyage was carried to the farthest extent when the alleged ulterior destination of the contraband cargo was applied to land transport as well. It was, at the same time, applied to blockaded port also if the intention was to send the cargo to blockaded port by the same ship or another one.

14. PORTUGAL *VS.* INDIA (1960)
[I.C.J. REPORTS (1960), 6]
(RIGHT OF PASSAGE OVER INDIAN TERRITORY)

This dispute arose between Portugal and India in 1954 when a revolt came to surface in Dadar and Nagar Haveli (now a Union Territory) against Portugese regime.

Portugal wanted to crush this revolt, but she could send her force to these places only through Indian territory. India denied her passage for sending troops. Portugal claimed the right of transit between Daman and the Portugese enclaves of Dadar and Nagar Haveli. Finally the case was referred to the International Court of Justice by the Government of Portugal in 1955.

Portugal claimed soverignty over Dadar and Nagar Haveli under the treaty of 1779 and claimed the right of passage as a customery practice. She charged India for violating international responsibility. India, however, denied any local custom for allowing passage to Portugal

The World Court's judgement went in favour of India. Its decision was based on the fact that the customary practice always demanded permission of the Indian Sovereign for the passage of Portugese armed forces. The Court held that Portugal had in 1954 a right of passage over the intervening Indian territory in respect of Private Persons, civil officials and goods to the extent claimed by Portugal but subject to regulation and control by India. An regards the passage of armed forces prior permission was necessary. The Soviet Judge even challenged the Court's jurisdiction, as portugal never had sovereign rights over the enclaves. In these circumstances the Court maintained that Indian refusal of passage was covered by its power of regulation and control of the right of passage exercised by Portugal. In other words, Portugal's right of passage was subject to full recognition and exercise of Indian Sovereignty over intervening territory and without any immunity in favour of Portugal.

15. CAMBODIA *VS.* THAILAND
[I.C.J. REPORTS 1926, P. 6]
(TERRITORIAL SOVEREIGNTY)

In this case Cambodia alleged a violation of its territorial sovereignty by Thailand over the region of the Temple of Preah Vihear and its precincts. But Thailand's contention was that the area in question was on the Thai side of the common frontier and so came under the sovereignty of Thailand.

The temple is an ancient sanctury and shrine situated on the border of both the countries. It is still a place of pilgrimage belonging to the eastern sector of the Dangrak range of mountains constituting the boundary in the region, Cambodia to the south and

Thailand to the north.

In 1949-50, a French note protested against 4 Siamese keepers found in the Temple which, however, remained unreplied by Thailand. Again, in 1953, Cambodia sent some guards to the Temple but finding Siamese keepers there, they withdrew and asked for explanation from the Thai Government. The fact of the matter was that even untill 1954 Thailand had not affirmed and territorial claim, although she had maintained her occuption by keeping troops there.

In 1983, a Conferrence was called between the two states at Bangkok, but the talk proved fruitless. Thailand did not challenge the map in which the Temple was shown to lie in Cambodian territory.

The case was subsequently referred to the World Court. The Court held that the Temple was situated in a territory which comes under Cambodian sovereignty, and Thailand was asked to withdraw her troops and to restore things removed from the Temple since 1954. This decision was based upon the interpretation of the boundary treaty (1907) between France and Siam and the subsequent conduct of Siam. In the maps prepared by the French topographical officers in accordance with the boundary treaty of 1907, Preah Vihear was shown on the Cambodian side and these maps were communicated to the Siamese Government but Siam had never raised any objection. Hence Thialand could not claim territorial sovereignty over the region under dispute.

16. NOTTEBOHM-LIECHTENSTEIN *VS.* GUATEMA LA (1955) [I.C.J. REPORTS (1955) 4] (NATIONALITY)

Nottebohm, a German national, owning land in Guatemala, left for Liechtenstein when Guatemala declared war against Germany. He was interned and his property was confiscated. In December 1951, Liechtenstein moved an application on behalf of Nottebohm alleged to be her national before the World Court.

Under Article 36, para 6 of the Statute, of the International Court of Justice the World Court first of all decided that it had jurisdiction in the case thereby over ruling the preliminary objection of Guatemala. The Court finally decided (1955) that Nottebohm was not a citizen of Liechtenstein. His naturalization with necessary conditions in Liechtenstein could not be proved. Nottebohm was to be treated as a citizen of Guatemala, because he had always retained his family links with Germany and Guatemala for the last 34 years and had no bond or attachment with Liechtenstein.

To Kunz, this judgement does not conform with international law on nationality. The criterion of 'genuine link' militates against the standing rules relating to nationality. It replaces a clear and objective criterion by a vague and subjective one. Moreover, under the new criterion a national is deprived of diplometic protection. Nevertheless, the concept of "effective nationality" or "genuine link" doctrine was followed by the UN Convention on Reduction of Statelessness (1961).

17. ALABAMA CLAMIS ARBITRATION (1872)
[(1872) I MOORE INTERNATIONAL ARBITRATION P. 653]
(NEUTRALITY)

During the American Civil War, a number of vessels were built in English shipyard for the use of Confederate Navy. The ship Alabma, built in English shipyards at liverpool, was unarmed when left liverpool, a British port. But, on her way she was supplied arms by some ships coming from England at the Azores which was a neutral territory situated in the North Atlantic ocean and belonged to Portugal. Further, the Alabama was expected to begin hostilities at once against the merchant ships of the USA. On the conclusion of Civil War, the US Government claimed compensation from England for the depradations caused to cruisers on account of the operation of the Alabama, but the British Government denied their responsiblity under International Law. The matter was ultimately referred to an arbitral tribunal under the Washington Treaty of 1871.

It was declared by the Tribunal that the constructing, arming and equipping of belligerentships in neutral waters or ports as bases of naval operations by the belligerents were prohibited. So all warlike operations of ships or men by the belligerents on neutral territories should be disallowed. In this case Britain was held liable and had to pay reparation amounting to $ 15,500,000 to the US.

18. IN RE ANGLO-IRANIAN OIL DISPUTE (1954)
(JURISDICTION OF I.C.J. IN RE INTERIM MEASURES)

The Anglo-Iranian Oil Company—a concern in which the British Government had a substantial interest—worked the extensive South Iranian oil fields. On May 1, 1951, the Majlis (Iranian Legislature) passed a law nationalizing its oil industry. Britain on behalf of the Company applied to International Court of Justice for provisional steps to preserve her rights in Iran until a decision was reached. In the mean time Iran ordered seizure of the installations.

The Court upheld the British plea for a freeze in the dispute maintaining that the previous arrangements should continue till the principal issue is decided. Both the parties should refrain from preventing the flow of oil It also recommended the appointment of a Joint Commission to keep oil moving and supervise the expenditure. But Iran formally rejected the ruling (concerning interim measures) of the World Court on July 8, 1951 on the ground that the Court had no jurisdiction in the dispute.

The Court's decision was subjected to criticism from many quarters. It had no power to pass an interim injunction since it could not permanently prevent the Government of Iran from nationalization. The Iranian Government took it as intervention in the internal affairs and considered it null and void. The two disenting Judges also observed that in these circumstances interim measures of protection should not have been indicated. The defiance of Iran did not add to the prestage of the Court. The dispute later was referred to the Security Council but its decision was deferred.

The I.C.J. finally on July 22, 1952 ruled that it was not competent to deal with the dispute. By 9 votes to 5 it decided that Iran did not violate international law by nationalizing the Company's 500 million Pounds sterling Persian properties.

19. DR DHARAM TEJA'S CASE (EXTRADITION)

The Jayanti Shipping Company was incorporated as a limited company with initial paid up capital of Rs 200. By 1962 its capital rose to Rs 15 million with 75 per cent share held by Dr Dharam Teja, who was originally a Physicist. Later on with the help of Nehru Dr. Teja wangled a loan of Rs 20 crore from the Indian Government.

By 1965 some criticism started in the Lok Sabha against the functioning of the Jayanti Company. The crux of the criticism was about fraudulent collection of concession, leakage of foreign exchange plus mismanagement. In June 1966, the Shastri Government took over the company for 5 years and entrusted it to the Shipping Corporation of India. Before any legal action could be taken Teja fled the country. A warrant for his arrest was issued by New Delhi Magistrate in 1967. Subsequently, Dr Teja along with his beautiful wife. Ranjit Kaur, were charged with criminal misappropriation of more than Rs 3 million in respect of Jayanti Shipping Company functioning under authorities of the Government of India in New York. The Indian Government demanded Teja's extradition from the Government of USA where both had escaped by 1967.

Teja's lawyer challanged the extradition treaties between the USA and Great Britain which was subsequently ractified by the Indian Government after independence. The lawyer for Indian Consulate in America presented a photostat copy of the said treaty pleading that it was in force between the USA and India as the present Government of India was beneficiary and successor to the extradition treaty under reference. The defence objection on behalf of Dr Teja was overruled by the commissioner for Southern district. The couple jumped bail from the New York Court and fled to Costa Rica, where they claimed diplomatic immunity. The Costa Rican Government, however, rejected the request of Dr Teja for political asylum. But at the same time it also turned down India's plea for extradition.

Dr Teja was ultimately run to ground at Heathrow airport in London in 1970. He was nabbed while leaving UK for Costa Rica, He claimed to be the personal representative of the President of Costa Rica. But he was produced before a Magistrate, Reginald Mandley, who signed a warrant to extradite Dr Teja. Teja was brought to India and put under trial on several charges. On 19 October 1972, he was sentenced to rigorous imprisonment for a term extending to three years and fines totalling Rs 14,30,000 on eight separate charges of criminal breach of trust, forgery and falsification of accounts of the Shipping Jayanti Company and was lodged in Tihar Jail by the Additional District and Session Judge, Mr M.L. Jain. His appeal was dismissed by the Delhi High Court in 1974.

During the period of emergency, however, Mr G. Murahari (Dy. Speaker of the Lok Sabha) and Mr Jagannath Rao (M.P.) helped Teja in setting accounts—in the literal sense—with the Government of Indian and obtained his release. Both were thus exonerated during the emergency and were released from Jail in late 1975 as remission in jail term was allowed. The significance of the case lies in the fact that it was the first case which revealed the relation of theory and practice of extradition to the law of state succession.

20. NORTH ATLANTIC COAST FISHERIES CASE (1970) [GREEN, INTERNATIONAL LAW THROUGH CASES (3RD EDITION, 1970) AT PP. 331 ET SEQ] (SERVITUDE AND ARBITRATION)

In the North Atlantic Coast Fisheries case the United States alleged that the fishery rights granted to her by Great Britain off the coast of Newfoundland under a treaty of 1818 were servitude. The Permanent Court of Arbitration did not agree with this contention on the ground that there was no evidence that the doctrine of international servitude was one with which either American or British statesmen were familier in 1818 and that the doctrine was unsuited to the principle of sovereignty and to the present international relations of sovereign states. The Court held that the right of Great Britain to make regulations without the consent of the United States to take fish was inherent to the sovereignty of Great Britain, which was limited in that the regulations must be made bonafied and must not be in violation of the treaty of 1818.

21. S.S. WIMBLEDON
[(1923) SERIES A NO. 1]
(TERRITORIAL JURISDICTION)

On 21 March 1921, the Wimbledon, a British vessel chartered by a French company, was refused access to the Kiel Canal by the German authorities on the ground that the vessel was carrying military materials to Poland which was then at War with Russia. The Permanent Court of International Justice held that it was the duty of Germany to have permitted the passage of Wimbledon through the Kiel Canal within the meaning of Article 380 of the Treaty of Versailles, which allowed a nation at peace with Germany a free passage through the Canal. German neutrality orders, therefore, were invalid. But the contention of Britain that the right of passing through the Kiel Canal was a State Servitude was not accepted by the Court. The Court observed that it was not called upon to take a definite attitude with regard to the question, which was of a very controversial nature, whether in the domain of international law, there really existed servitudes analogous to the servitudes of private law.

Following the two cases cited above in which the doctrine of international servitude was rejected, the opinion is growing among authorities that it is not really a necessary doctrine in the international field and hence can be dispensed with.

In this connection, the following comment by Lauterpacht is in point:

"Of all attempts to apply to relations between states conceptions taken from private law, none has caused more confusion or has brought the recourse to analogy into more disrepute than the efforts made to introduce the conception of servitudes into Public International Law."

22. ALTMARK (1940)
[HACKWORTH, DIGEST VII, 568]
(NEUTRILITY)

This German auxiliary vessel was carrying out 300 British Officers and Sailors taken from a number of British merchantships sunk by a German warship. When Altmark entered the Norwegian territorial waters on its way from South America to Germany, a British destroyer, Cossack, released the British prisoners and took them to England in spite of the Norwegian Government's protest on the ground of violation of its neutrility. The British Government argued that the rule of free passage through territorial waters was not applicable because of the presence of prisoners on Altmark. But ultimately the Norwegian Government's contention that Altmark being a warship was exempt from search and was entitled to passage through neutral territory in spite of the presence of prisoners on board the ship was found in accordance with Article 10 of the Hague Convention XIII (1907).

23. THE APPAM
[HUDSON CASES, 1352]
(NEUTRALITY)

A German Cruiser had captured the Appam, a British merchant vessel, and brought it on February 1, 1916 to the port of Norfolk (USA), although the US was nentral. Libel proceedings were started against the Appam on the ground that her presence was in violation of the US neutrality. The Supreme Court of United States held that the effort to make of an American port a depository of captured vessels for an indefinite period was a breach of neutrality within the traditional policy of the US and the Provisons of the Hague Conventions on the Rights and Duties of neutral powers in naval war.

24. FRANCISKA (1855)
[10 MOO P.C., 36]
(BLOCKADE)

The Franciska was a Danish vessel, which was captured by a British Cruiser when she was no her way to Riga (Russia), a port blockaded by Britain during the Crimean War against Russia. During this war various orders were issued by the British, French and Russian Governments, the effect of which was to permit trade to be carried on by their respective subjects in the Baltic ports. These ports were blockaded by the British and French fleets, but the orders had the effect of excluding neutrals from such trade.

It was contended on behalf of the owners of the ship that there was no intention to break the blockade, and she was ordered to proceed to Riga only if there was no blockade.

The Privy Council held that the blockaded place must be watched by a force sufficient to render the egress and ingress dangerous and that the plea of ignorance of the existence of the blockade in the particular case was invalid because the captain of the ship was aware of the blockade when the ship sailed from the last port. Their Lordships of the Judicial Committee, however, held that as the blockade was relaxed in favour of belligerents to the exclusion of neutrals, it was not a legal blockade, and, therefore, the vessel was improperly seized for attempting to enter the port of Riga and must be restored.

25. In Re Castioni (1890)
[Law Reports (1891) Q.B.D. p. 149]
(Extradition)
(See Chapter 13

26. In Re Meunier (1894)
[Law Reports (1894) 1 Q B.D., p. 415]
(Extradition)
[See Chapter 13]

27. Savarker's Case
[1911 No. IX]
(Extradition)
[See Chapter 13]

28. Eisler's Extradition Case
[Tandon, M.P., Pub. International Law, Allahabad, —Allahabad Law Agency, 15th edn. 1976 p., 649]
(Extradition)
[See Chapter 13]

29. In Re Kolezynsnski & Other s
[(1955) All E.R. 31]
(Extradition)
[See Chapter 13]

30. Adolf Eichman Case
[District Court of Jerusalem, Judgment of Dec. 11, 1961]

(Jurisdiction and Extradition)
[See Chapter 13]

31. Tarasov's Extradition Case
[Tandon, M.P., Pub. International Law, Alld. Allahabad Law Agency, 15th edition, 1976, p. 651]
(See Chapter 13)

32. North Sea Conitineta l Shelf Case
[I.C.J. Reports, 1969, p. 3]
(Continental Shelf Areas in the North Sea-Delimitation between adjacent States)
[See chapter 8]

33. The Caroline (1839)
[Moore, Digest, II, s. 217]
(Doctrine of Self-Defence)
[See Chapter 10]

34. Daimler Co. Ltd. *VS.* Continental Tyre and Rubber Co. Ltd. (Great Britain)
[(1916) 2 A.C. 307]
(Enemy Character)
[See Chapter 19]

35. USA. *VS.* Rauscher
[(1886) (119 US 407]
(Extradition)
[See Chapter 13]

Index